*Twayne's English Authors Series*

*Thomas Babington Macaulay*

**TEAS 217**

Thomas Babington Macaulay

# THOMAS BABINGTON MACAULAY

By MARGARET CRUIKSHANK

TWAYNE PUBLISHERS

A DIVISION OF G. K. HALL & CO., BOSTON

**Library of Congress Cataloging in Publication Data**

Cruikshank, Margaret.
  Thomas Babington Macaulay.

  Bibliography: p. 165–71
  Includes index.
  (Twayne's English authors series ; TEAS 217)
  1. Macaulay, Thomas Babington Macaulay, Baron
  1800–1859—Criticism and interpretation.

  PR4963.C7      828'.8'09      77-10906
  ISBN 0-8057-6686-3

To the memory of
Louise Wimmer Cruikshank
and to
George Cruikshank

# Contents

# *About the Author*

Margaret L. Cruikshank, a native of northern Minnesota and a graduate of the College of St. Scholastica, holds a Ph.D. in English from Loyola University. She has taught at Loyola, Rosary College, Central College, St. John's University, and Mankato State University. In 1975, she established a women's studies program at Mankato State, which she directed for two years. She has written articles about Macaulay, Victorian women writers, recent feminist writing, and women's studies, and has also published several short autobiographical sketches.

# Preface

This study is an introduction to Thomas Babington Macaulay, the last of the major Victorian prose writers to be reevaluated. Although I give some background information and relate Macaulay to the Victorian age, my focus is on several important works. There are few models for analyzing nonfiction prose texts. I have examined the form of some individual works, considering the kinds of questions that are raised about poems, plays, and novels, because several of Macaulay's best works have not been studied for their intrinsic literary merit. At the same time, I have tried to explain Macaulay's ideas, the assumptions underlying his writing, and the connections among his works, because his prose, like Victorian prose generally, deals with public issues. His poetry, which is far less significant than his prose, is not included here.

Since criticism of Macaulay has tended until recently to be rather disparaging, I emphasize his strengths as a writer. To give an impression of the vigor of his prose style, I quote him freely. The excerpts should also illustrate his sense of humor.

The introduction gives an overview of Macaulay. Five chapters are devoted to his essays because readers are more likely to begin with them than with the *History of England* and because differences among the essays need to be stressed. Chapters 2 and 4 deal with argumentative strategy in the essays. In Chapter 5, I relate Macaulay's idea of the historical essay to "Lord Clive." His literary criticism and method of writing literary history are treated in Chapter 6, which is primarily a study of the essays on Fanny Burney and Addison. Chapter 7 describes the biographical articles Macaulay wrote for the *Encyclopaedia Britannica*. Because he was known for his role in Indian affairs as well as for his writing, I consider the Minute on Indian Education in a separate chapter. Macaulay's major work, the *History of England*, is examined in Chapter 8. It is elucidated to some extent by earlier chapters as well, since many generalizations about the essays apply equally to the *History*. Chapter 9 is devoted to Macaulay's parliamentary speeches. His literary reputation is considered in Chapter 10. The conclusion suggests why Macaulay can be read enjoyably today.

Two of the finest works of recent Victorian scholarship were published after I began this book, John Clive's *Macaulay: the Shaping of the Historian* and Thomas Pinney's edition of Macaulay's letters. My book was nearly completed by the time I read the excellent studies of Macaulay by Jane Millgate and Joseph Hamburger.

I wish to thank Professor Martin J. Svaglic of Loyola University, Chicago, who directed my dissertation and taught me the importance of argument in Victorian prose. A grant from the research council of Central College, Pella, Iowa, helped me gather materials for this book. For a fellowship that enabled me to begin writing, I am very grateful to the Institute for Ecumenical and Cultural Research, Collegeville, Minnesota. The staffs of Alcuin Library, St. John's University, Collegeville, and Wilson Library, University of Minnesota, have been most helpful. I owe special thanks to University of Minnesota reference librarian Sandy Allen and to friends who read early drafts of my chapters: Mary Catherine Cruikshank, Elizabeth O'Dell, Robert O'Dell, Susan Ebbers, Susan Hill, Edward Jones, Ruth Jones, Arthur Johnson, Judith Niemi, Pat Cruikshank Parthé, Molly Taylor, Richard Taylor, and Judith Turcott.

MARGARET L. CRUIKSHANK

*Duluth, Minnesota*

# Chronology

1800   Thomas Babington Macaulay born October 25 at Rothley Temple, Leicestershire.

1813   Leaves family home at Clapham to attend private school.

1818   Enters Trinity College, Cambridge.

1823   Begins writing for *Knight's Quarterly*.

1824   Becomes fellow of Trinity; makes first public speech.

1825   Contributes first essays to *Edinburgh Review*.

1830   Elected to House of Commons for Calne.

1831   Becomes known for speeches supporting Reform Bill.

1832   Elected to House of Commons for Leeds.

1834   Goes to India as legal member of Supreme Council.

1835   Minute on Indian Education.

1837   Indian Penal Code.

1838   Returns from India.

1839   Elected to House of Commons for Edinburgh; made secretary at war in Melbourne's cabinet.

1842   *Lays of Ancient Rome.*

1843   *Critical and Historical Essays Contributed to the Edinburgh Review.*

1844   Writes last *Edinburgh Review* essay.

1846   Reelected for Edinburgh; appointed paymaster general in Russell's cabinet.

1847   Defeated in Edinburgh election.

1848   *History of England*, volumes I and II.

1852   Reelected for Edinburgh; suffers heart attack and never fully recovers.

1853   Delivers last speech in House of Commons; begins biographies for *Encyclopaedia Britannica*.

1854   *Speeches.*

1855   *History of England*, volumes III and IV.

1856   Resigns seat in House of Commons.

1857   Becomes Lord Macaulay (Baron Macaulay of Rothley).

1858   Writes last *Encyclopaedia Britannica* article.
1859   Macaulay dies December 28.
1861   *History of England*, volume V.

### CHAPTER 1

# Introduction

THE works of Thomas Babington Macaulay were once as widely read as the novels of Charles Dickens. One hundred years ago, travelers to Australia found in every squatter's hut a copy of Macaulay's *Essays*, alongside Shakespeare and the Bible. When he died, *The Times* described him as "the most powerful, popular, and versatile writer of our time,"[1] but today Macaulay is relatively neglected. Readers who can easily identify Mr. Micawber have only a vague notion of another famous Victorian character, Macaulay's schoolboy, made famous by the phrase "every schoolboy knows," which the writer used to drive his points home. Macaulay may never again be as popular as Dickens, but he deserves a wider audience than he has had in recent decades. An examination of his writing will show that he is both a powerful and a versatile writer.

## I  *Life*

Macaulay's hypothetical schoolboy is easily likened to Macaulay himself. If the schoolboy knew that Cortez imprisoned Montezuma and that Pizarro strangled Atahualpa,[2] Macaulay, as a child, knew a great deal more. Born October 25, 1800, St. Crispin's day, at Rothley Temple, an uncle's home in Leicestershire, Thomas Babington Macaulay was the son of Selina Mills and Zachary Macaulay, editor of the *Christian Observer*. The family lived in London, where Macaulay spent most of his life. By the time he was eight, he had planned an outline of world history beginning with the creation, attempted imitations of Virgil and Sir Walter Scott, and written an essay designed to convert heathens to Christianity. This last effort strongly suggests the influence of Zachary, but the son's independence was foretold in 1816 when the elder Macaulay, who compared novel reading to "drinking drams in the morning,"[3] printed an anonymous defense of fiction that not only offended readers by its praise of Henry Fielding and Tobias Smollett, but turned out to be the work of his own son.

Macaulay's early love of Fielding is noteworthy for several reasons. He was an enthusiastic novel reader all his life; he aimed to make history as interesting as fiction; and an eighteenth century spirit pervades his work. Like the novelist, Macaulay had a strong sense of the ludicrous. Another trait common to Fielding and Macaulay, ascribed by the later writer to Oliver Cromwell, is a "masculine and full-grown robustness of mind [which] has peculiarly characterized the great men of England" ("Hallam," *Works*, VII, 292). Macaulay assuredly was one of the great men of Victorian England.

Zachary Macaulay, an important public figure, made his special cause the abolition of slavery. Since he and other Evangelical reformers lived in the village of Clapham, outside London, their circle became known as the "Clapham Sect" or "the Saints." Tom Macaulay grew up hearing political issues debated with righteous fervor. From his mother came a great love for literature. Selina Macaulay had been educated by Hannah More, a famous survivor of the age of Samuel Johnson, who often entertained Macaulay when he was a child and planned to leave him her library. Later, when Selina wanted to send Hannah More, a staunch Tory like Johnson, a copy of a pro-Reform speech made by Tom, he protested, "If you do, she'll cut me off with a prayerbook" (Trevelyan, I, 170). Macaulay had a special love for his mother, but his love of his two youngest sisters, Hannah and Margaret, was extraordinarily intense. For this reason, perhaps, he never married, although after Hannah married Charles Trevelyan, he was happily absorbed into her family life. Her son, George Otto Trevelyan, became Macaulay's biographer.

Few precocious childhoods have been followed by careers as brilliant as those Macaulay pursued, from a Cambridge fellowship to political and literary triumphs culminating in a peerage. As a young man he was famous both for his *Edinburgh Review* articles and his speeches in the House of Commons supporting the Reform Bill, which extended the vote and gave parliamentary representation to the great industrial towns of England. As an Indian administrator in the 1830s, Macaulay was known for his Minute on Indian Education and the Indian Penal Code. Three publications in the following decade were among the most popular works of the nineteenth century: Macaulay's poems, *The Lays of Ancient Rome;* his collected *Edinburgh* essays; and the first part of his *History of England.* Although the popularity of the 1825 essay on John Milton prompted Trevelyan to compare his uncle's sudden fame with Lord Byron's, the *History* established even more firmly Macaulay's place as one of the great figures of his time. After suffering a heart attack in 1852, he could not work as energetically as he had all his life, but continued historical research and in the last years of his life wrote five short biographies for the *Encyclopaedia Britannica.* He became Lord Macaulay in 1857. Weakened by poor health and overwhelmed by the expected loss of Hannah, who was to join her husband in India, he died in 1859. He was buried in Westminster Abbey.

## II  *Major Works*

Macaulay's greatest success, and the work for which he hoped to be remembered, is the *History of England from the Accession of James II*. Three thousand copies were sold in the first ten days after it appeared in 1848. A formidably long work, more often alluded to than read in its entirety, like *The Faerie Queene* and *Middlemarch*, Macaulay's *History* has served as a symbol of Victorian England. It is a monument as well as a document, however, and catalogues of its "Victorian" qualities obscure the fact that it is a remarkable composition, sometimes likened to an epic or a drama, which covers the period 1685 to 1702, the reigns of James II and William of Orange. It can be described as Whig history, narrative history, political and social history, but the labels do not indicate the scope and complexity of the work, which reflects both eighteenth century attitudes and the influence of Romanticism.

The first is the more obvious. Macaulay echoes Edward Gibbon in the preface to the *History* by stating that he will describe not only the growth of English power and wealth but "great national crimes and follies" (*Works*, I, 2). The formal, public style of the preface is maintained throughout. Macaulay's tone is detached; he does not share the Romantic view of writing as self-expression. Even when he uses emotional language, Macaulay appeals less to the man of feeling than the man of common sense, or the "plain man," as he is called in one essay. In the *History*, Macaulay extols reason and moderation as well as common sense. Finally, he uses a rhetorical device common in eighteenth century literature—antithesis—to form individual sentences and, on a larger scale, to present ideas and develop characters.

As an historical work revealing a Romantic spirit, the *History of England* is not in the same category as Carlyle's *French Revolution*, a subjective, poetical meditation on great events, but Romanticism in Macaulay should not be ignored. If the stately manner of Gibbon influenced him, so too did the vivid pages of Scott. Macaulay's great love of the past, especially of its picturesque qualities, is clearly a Romantic trait. Fond of day dreaming and castle building, he delighted in imagining himself taking part in memorable scenes of the past.[4] Another link to Romanticism is Macaulay's curiosity about the impact of great events upon the lives of ordinary people, shown by the famous third chapter of the *History*, "England in 1685," an early example of social history.

The essays cover a large part of Macaulay's career, from the time he was an obscure Cambridge graduate with neither the wealth nor the aristocratic ties required to succeed in politics, to the time he was a distinguished statesman in the cabinet of Lord Melbourne. The essays were so popular that by 1876 Trevelyan could boast that the market for them "falls and rises with the general prosperity of the nation [so that] the demand for Macaulay varies with the demand for coal" (II, 72). Macaulay would have approved of the analogy.

The usual division of these works, which follows the title of the 1843 collection *Critical and Historical Essays Contributed to the Edinburgh Review*, is not very helpful. The essays are sometimes both critical and historical ("Addison") or polemical and historical ("Hallam"). A more useful classification can be based upon the purpose of the essays rather than their subjects. Their aims are to persuade or to describe, and the emphasis in each work is usually clear. Thus the essays can be divided into argumentative and narrative works.[5] In the essay on Milton, for example, the description of Milton's life is subordinated to an argumentative end, justifying the poet's public conduct. Specific points are debated in the essays on Robert Clive and Warren Hastings, but these works are primarily narrative. Two essays treating the same periods of English history have very different endings: Macaulay concludes "Hallam" by advocating the Whig case for the Reform Bill, a case implicitly defended by his selection and interpretation of events in the review; the essay on the Whig historian James Mackintosh, on the other hand, evokes the revolutionary period for its intrinsic interest and ends abruptly with an exhortation to read Mackintosh.

Classification of the essays as arguments and narratives, which should provide a better context for discussions of style than the critical-historical division, is suggested by a letter Macaulay wrote in 1832 to Macvey Napier, the *Edinburgh* editor, after finishing the essay on John Hampden: "It is in part a narrative. This is a sort of composition which I have never yet attempted."[6] Since the essays written between 1825 and 1832 are argumentative, and since most of the essays after 1832 are narrative, this classification fits a general chronological order. A survey of Macaulay's works will show that his talent was better suited to narration than to argument. Although readers have preferred the narratives, the characteristic excellences of these works have not been adequately demonstrated by critics. In their zeal to write "typically Victorian" in large letters across the pages of Macaulay, critics have tended to overlook the merits of his individual works.

The parliamentary speeches bring out an important aspect of Macaulay, his humanitarian spirit. Although many speeches treat subjects of little interest to the general reader—army allocations, for example, and a bill to prevent railway travel on Sunday (opposed by Macaulay)—those that deal with such topics as state aid to education, discrimination against minorities, and violence in Ireland are clearly relevant today. To some extent the speeches reflect Victorian blindspots—an identification of lower class interests with those of the middle class, for example—but Macaulay's speeches, like his better known works, display a remarkable command of language. Even an unpromising subject like factory legislation becomes transformed, through his eloquence, into a classic exposition of the state's duties toward its citizens.

A strong sense of England's responsibilities toward her Indian subjects underlies the education minute (1835), parts of which will sound chauvinistic to the modern reader. The minute expresses both a practical approach to governing and an idealistic faith in the civilizing power of education. Most Victorians shared Macaulay's belief in education as improvement, but he was ahead of his time in seeing the importance of secular education, which he ably defends in an early essay, "The London University."

The image of Macaulay conveyed by survey texts, literary histories, and anthologies has often been very negative. He has been
seen as an anti-intellectual materialist, a narrow Whig, and a fierce
partisan (one chapter of R. C. Beatty's 1938 biography is titled
"Hater"). He has been called smug, complacent, unfeeling, and
shallow, and has been portrayed as a man who never developed.
Fortunately for Macaulay's reputation, the limitation of these
stereotypes is proven by recent studies.[7] Unfavorable opinion has
some justification, but often results from generalizations based upon
only a few of Macaulay's many works. The charge of anti-
intellectualism rests on some statements in one of forty reviews,
"Bacon." Certain passages in other essays do sound very smug indeed, but out of context their rhetorical purpose cannot be understood. Shallowness can be found in some of the early writings, in the
treatment of James Boswell in the first Johnson essay for example.
And Macaulay's development is not obvious; he left no record of it
such as *Sartor Resartus* or *Apologia Pro Vita Sua*. But when attention shifts from Macaulay the "preeminent Victorian"[8] to the characteristics of his works, his merit is clearer.

### III   *Some Characteristics*

Of many characteristics of Macaulay that can be pointed out to the
reader approaching his works for the first time, three of the most
important are his many-sidedness, his moderation, and his love of
the past.

Now that scholars have re-evaluated the Victorian period, the
label "Victorian" no longer serves as a complete description of a
writer. The many sides of Macaulay, clear from the pages of Trevelyan, are more fully shown by Clive. The appearance of both conservative and radical attitudes in his works, for example, can be related
to his "Whiggish eclecticism" and to his temperament, which was
"naturally attuned to paradox, iconoclasm, and the unexpected"[9]
Like others from Evangelical families who rejected the stern
moralism and repression of their childhoods, Macaulay sometimes
attacked institutionalized Christianity, but he often defended Christian values.

The most vehement of his reviews show him to be a great fighter,
but that is only one side to Macaulay. Readers of Trevelyan saw a
gentle, playful, and whimsical man, who described parliamentary
events in satirical letters to his sisters, and who could amuse himself

by making up games for his nieces and nephews. The strength of his emotions was not apparent to those who knew him only in his public role. Famous at twenty-five as a writer and at thirty-one as an orator, he became a great historian before he was fifty. Poet, historian, reviewer, Indian legislator, politician, Macaulay was also a brilliant talker and a very good letter writer.

Since he was a great lover of classical literature throughout his life, it is not surprising that the classical ideal of moderation in all things should have appealed to Macaulay. Fanaticism of any kind repelled him. He occasionally praised men who avoided theological controversy by likening them to Allworthy seated between Thwackum and Square, a significant comparison because of the three characters from *Tom Jones,* only Allworthy *acts* virtuously. Both the Tories' dread of innovation and the Utilitarians' contempt for traditional values struck him as dangerous extremes.

Macaulay's moderation impressed one contemporary, who wrote in his diary after a meeting in 1826, "His opinions are quite liberal and yet he is by no means a vulgar radical."[10] Thus moderation is apparent not only in what he says but in his manner of saying it. A characteristic method in his reviews is to describe extremes so that the superiority of the middle course can be emphasized. A certain mistrust of theories results from Macaulay's moderation, but his love of the classics is proof that this distrust did not make him anti-intellectual. "The business of a Member of Parliament," he wrote to Leeds voters in 1832, "is the pursuit not of speculative truth, but of practical good."[11] Neither was the pursuit of speculative truth Macaulay's business as an essayist or historian. The "message" of his works is much less the message of progress or Whig righteousness than the wisdom of moderation.

Another characteristic of Macaulay is that nearly all of his works deal with the past, either directly, through summaries and interpretations of events, or indirectly, through discussion of a contemporary event in the light of historical parallels. In a sense, the present interests Macaulay only as it reflects history; and, consequently, his view of the present is often abstract. The factory system, for example, which caused great suffering to individuals, symbolized for him the progress of the nation as a whole. Thus the system's theoretical benefits impressed him more than its practical evils, the exploitation of children, for example. Reform in order to preserve, one of his great principles, upheld a political goal consistent with past experience. Much of the appeal of Macaulay's essays lies in his ability to communicate his love of the past to his readers. At a time when the reading public was greatly increasing, his sketches created interest in the past. The aphorisms and lively commonplaces with which he entertains the reader show a wide knowledge of men and politics. The talent for saying what is ordinary and familiar in impressive language has often been identified as one source of his appeal.

Macaulay celebrates England's past in his *History*, essays, and speeches. He had a special fondness for eighteenth century literature and politics, and some of his best essays—"Clive," "William Pitt," "Addison"—treat eighteenth century figures. Trevelyan wrote that "Macaulay's youth was nourished upon Pope, and Bolingbroke, and Atterbury, and Defoe. . . . He knew every pamphlet which had been put forth by Swift, or Steele, or Addison" (II, 368–69). The advantage of this immersion for a literary historian is obvious, but Macaulay's love of the past had a concomitant disadvantage: it kept him from appreciating the most creative writers among his contemporaries. That "he was not fond of new lights," is one of the few shortcomings that Trevelyan attributes to his uncle (II, 382).

Macaulay's absorption in history led him to reflect upon the reasons for England's greatness. The most important of these become his chief themes: progress and liberty. "The history of England is emphatically the history of progress," he wrote in 1835, progress visible in the "moral, intellectual, and physical state" of Englishmen in the nineteenth century ("Mackintosh," *Works*, VIII, 442–43). Famous passages in Macaulay extol material progress, but as this passage demonstrates, he does not confine progress to new inventions and the increase of wealth.

What exactly does Macaulay mean by moral and intellectual improvement? He believed that while circumstances change, human nature remains the same. His great stress on liberty helps to resolve an apparent contradiction here. The security of political and religious liberty in the nineteenth century, compared to earlier times, furnished Macaulay with impressive evidence for moral and intellectual progress. To understand his works, one must see the interconnection of the progress and liberty themes. In "Mackintosh," the link between them is especially emphasized. Many passages throughout his works describing the struggle between oppression and freedom are overlooked in conventional treatments of Macaulay as the archetypal Victorian optimist; but the importance of these passages is stressed by a nineteenth century critic, John Morley, in one of the best essays on Macaulay. "The commonplaces of patriotism and freedom would never have been so powerful in Macaulay's hands," he noted, "if they had not been inspired by a sincere and hearty faith in them in the soul of the writer."[12]

A more common judgment is that Macaulay's writing is memorable for its style; his ideas are usually disparaged, notably his idea of progress. Many passages in George Eliot and J. S. Mill reflect their belief in progress, but they are not scored for optimism. If Macaulay's statements on progress had been less exuberant, the *idea* of progress would not be so readily joined to his name.

## IV *Style*

Morley wrote that Macaulay's style should not be considered in the narrow sense of "the grammar and mechanism of writing," but in relation to what he called "the temper or conscience of the intellect."[13] How can this distinction be observed in a study of Macaulay? One way is to treat whole works. In a lecture that marked the hundredth anniversary of Macaulay's birth, the classical scholar R. C. Jebb cautioned that Macaulay's "style" could not be distinguished from "incidental uses of rhetoric" if his writings were read in abridgements.[14] The structure of a complete work reflects its style. Thus, the ways Macaulay divides a work can illustrate the temper of his intellect. His prose style is not elegant, but its clarity is impressive. He took more trouble than most writers to be clear. The first rule of writing, he assures Macvey Napier, "is that the words used by the writer shall be such as most fully and precisely convey his meaning. . . . All considerations about the purity and dignity of style ought to bend to this consideration (18 April 1842; Trevelyan, II, 56). Macaulay's practice conforms very well to this rule. For clarity he chooses emphatic words and phrases, antithesis, and hyperbole—incidental uses of rhetoric to consider before turning to individual works.

The authoritative tone of Macaulay's writing comes partly from emphatic words. The following example describes the fate of Machiavelli's books. They "were misrepresented by the learned, misconstrued by the ignorant, censured by the church, abused, with all the rancour of simulated virtue, by the tools of a base government and the priests of a baser superstition" (*Works*, VII,

113). The increasing emphasis is clear when paralleled words are listed separately:

|                |                    |
|----------------|--------------------|
| misrepresented | base government    |
| misconstrued   | baser superstition |
| censured       |                    |
| abused         |                    |

Particularly in early works, Macaulay also uses a great number of superlatives and exclusive expressions of this kind from "Machiavelli":

> the *whole* people
> *all* the causes
> *every* man and who has seen the world
> *every* age and *every* nation
> *nothing* was ever written.

For Macaulay, antithesis is more than a way of arranging words and sentences; it is a way of perceiving, one that reflects a strong affinity for order and balance. When his antithetical patterns are rigid his writing lacks, in Matthew Arnold's phrase, "the soft play of life,"[15] but Arnold's generalization more accurately describes the early essays than the late essays or the *Encyclopaedia Britannica* articles. The frequent use of antithetical sentences also reveals Macaulay's habit of reducing complex ideas or the various aspects of a problem to fairly simple dichotomies. "The difference between the soaring angel and the creeping snake," he wrote in one of his best known works, "was but a type of the difference between Bacon the philosopher and Bacon the Attorney-general" (VIII, 552). This summary of William Pitt's career, written many years after the Bacon essay, shows a greater sense of complexity, however:

History will vindicate the real man . . . and will exhibit him as what he was, a minister of great talents, honest intentions, and liberal opinions, pre-eminently qualified, intellectually and morally, for the part of a parliamentary leader, and capable of administering, with prudence and moderation, the government of a prosperous and tranquil country, but unequal to surprising and terrible emergencies, and liable, in such emergencies, to err grievously, both on the side of weakness and on the side of violence. (X, 563–64)

A breakdown of this long sentence shows Macaulay's fondness for parallel constructions:

```
minister
  of great talents
    honest intentions
    liberal opinions
  qualified
    intellectually
    morally
  capable                    but unequal to emergencies
    prudence                 liable to err
    moderation                 both on the side of weakness
                               and on the side of violence
```

Antithetical sentence patterns are well suited to expressing Macaulay's favorite themes: the action-reaction movement of history, the transformation from a rude age to a polished age, and the struggle between freedom and tyranny. Moreover, antithesis imparts a special force to his aphorisms. Emphasizing his preference for the concrete and practical to the theoretical, for example, he declares that "an acre in Middlesex is better than a principality in Utopia" (VIII, 614). Since Macaulay's imagery is simple and is drawn from natural processes—sowing and reaping, the ebb and flow of the tide—it lends itself to antithetical patterns.

Macaulay's paragraphs often expand a single thought through many antithetical phrases and sentences. An example is a two page paragraph in "Mackintosh" that begins, "The history of England is emphatically the history of progress." The paragraph moves from the twelfth century to the nineteenth, and identifies in its climax the struggle for the Reform Bill as a higher stage of the old clash between tyranny and freedom. Contrasting the "wretched and degraded race" that the English once were to the "highly civilised people" they have become, Macaulay demonstrates that history's cyclic changes bring progress (VIII, 442–44). The back and forth movement of this paragraph and its rise to a climax suggest the same meaning. One reason the late essays appear more compact than earlier works is that sweeping paragraphs of the kind described here are less common in them.

Macaulay's frequent use of contrast as an organizing principle for works and parts of works corresponds to his antithetical sentence patterns. The main figures of the *History*, James and William, are contrasted throughout the work as representatives of attitudes hostile to English liberty on the one hand, and favorable to it on the other. "History," an essay written in 1828, is structured on two large contrasts: ancient history versus modern, and history as it should be written versus history as it has been written. "Southey's Colloquies" and "Mill on Government" are unified by an implicit contrast between the right way to view government and wrong ways: Robert Southey's approach is too imaginative; Mill's is not imaginative enough. The idea that poetry declines with the advance of civilization is elaborated in "Milton" and again in "Dryden."

In the Byron essay, Macaulay argues that the stark contrasts used by the historian to draw character are inappropriate for the dramatist because they produce "not a man, but a personified epigram" (VII, 560). Because of their exaggerations, some of Macaulay's own portraits are open to the same charge, those of Samuel Johnson and Horace Walpole, for example. When his sister Hannah questioned his insight into character, he retorted, in a letter to Hannah and another sister, Margaret: "If she knew how far I see into her she would be ready to hang herself" (2 August 1832; Pinney, II, 167). As antithetical sentences reflect Macaulay's desire for order, the tendency to exaggerate can be related to his high spirits.

The love of exaggeration appeared early. Attending a birthday party when he was eight, Tom Macaulay corrected Marianne Thornton, one of his Clapham neighbors, when she said that Napoleon would invade England and cut down the tree in her yard. He assured the girl that Napoleon planned instead to "stab all the little children in their beds."[16] Both as a child and an adult, Macaulay felt strongly the drama and excitement of the past, and that is one reason why exaggerated statements are fairly common in his writing.[17] Another is his belief that a periodical writer must make a vivid first impression on readers, since his articles will probably not be read a second time. Often dismissed as violations of truth when they are quoted out of context, Macaulay's exaggerations can be seen in another way, as parts of a whole, when an entire work is read. Macaulay uses exaggeration deliberately. The best portraits, he says in the essay on Machiavelli, contain an element of caricature, and the best historical accounts are "those in which a little of the exaggeration of fictitious narrative is judiciously employed. Something is lost in accuracy; but much is gained in effect. The fainter lines are neglected; but the great characteristic features are imprinted on the mind forever" (VII, 112). The last sentence succinctly describes Macaulay's early writing: the fainter lines are indeed neglected, but the great characteristic features are imprinted with remarkable clarity. In the *History,* the late *Edinburgh* articles, and the *Encyclopaedia* essays, more attention is paid to the fainter lines.

We know from Clive's *Macaulay: the Shaping of the Historian* that Macaulay's life was not as happy as Trevelyan portrayed it; yet compared to other Victorian writers, he seemed to live tranquilly, perhaps because his fame, won early, never diminished. With his attention focused on the past, he remained undisturbed by the rapid and sometimes violent changes taking place in his own day. He urged various reforms, but ultimately had no quarrel with his age; and his prose reflects this satisfaction. The works of other Victorians have found a more receptive audience in the twentieth century. But Macaulay, complacent as he occasionally sounds, has much pleasure and stimulation to offer readers who can imaginatively enter a world where reason guides human affairs and where technological progress is exciting rather than threatening; and who can share his belief that the great public benefactors are moderates rather than extremists.

CHAPTER 2

# "Southey's Colloquies" and "Civil Disabilities of the Jews"

## I Edinburgh *Essays 1825–1831*

AT the time Macaulay became a fellow of Trinity College, Cambridge, in 1824, he was already contributing essays, sketches, and poems to *Knight's Quarterly* and would soon begin writing for the leading Whig journal, the *Edinburgh Review*. The *Edinburgh* articles impressed a wealthy Whig, who offered Macaulay a seat in Parliament. He was elected in 1830, in time to take part in the historic debates on the Reform Bill, which he ardently supported even though it abolished his seat. Macaulay's first *Edinburgh* essays foreshadow his pro-Reform speeches, but his subjects are literature and history as well as politics.

The following reviews treat politics: "The West Indies" (1825) and "Social and Industrial Capacities of Negroes" (1827), two antislavery essays; "The London University" (1826), an argument for extending university education to the middle class; "The Present Administration" (1827), a defense of George Canning's coalition government;[1] three essays on Utilitarianism (1829), of which the most important is a reply to James Mill's *Essay on Government;* "Southey's Colloquies" (1830), a spirited attack on the Tory views of the poet laureate; two essays on population (1830, 1831); and "Civil Disabilities of the Jews" (1831), a plea for granting full citizenship to English Jews. These writers are subjects of early *Edinburgh* articles: Milton (1825), Machiavelli (1827), Dryden (1828), Montgomery (1830), Byron (1830), Bunyan (1831), and Johnson (1831). The long reviews "History" and "Hallam," both written in 1828, are the only works dealing exclusively with history, but historical questions are discussed in other early essays, the English Civil War in "Milton," for example.

Although the interweaving of politics, literature, and history in these reviews gives them an impressive diversity, a unifying element can be found in their argumentative tone. Some works are more clearly polemical then others, but issues are debated in all of them, even in those few that like "Bunyan," are more expository than argumentative. Macaulay did not expect these reviews to survive, but the 1843 collection of them, *Critical and Historical Essays*, became one of the most popular works of the nineteenth century, in the United States as well as in England.

When Macaulay defends Canning's government by saying that it upholds "freedom of worship, of discussion, and of trade,"[2] he summarizes the political judgments of the early reviews: the statement connects free trade, a tenet of laissez-faire liberalism, with liberty. Macaulay's belief in restricted government power links him to modern conservatives, his great emphasis on freedom to modern liberals. In the early essays he characteristically attacks what he takes to be extreme political positions, such as the justification of oppression in the case of slavery; or a foolish acceptance of the status quo shown by opponents of the new London University. Similarly, he defends the Reform Bill as a compromise between those who wanted no change and those who favored universal suffrage. In describing past events, Macaulay often says that England's greatness depended partly on the success of timely compromises. To Tories and radicals, this "Whig via media" merely demonstrated a lack of principle, but it could be seen far more positively as a safeguard against fanaticism.[3]

Another label, "Utilitarian," is useful if qualified. Macaulay is certainly closer to the Utilitarians, who were also called Philosophic Radicals, than to the Tories; he agrees that the end of government is the greatest good of the greatest number, and his legal reforms in India show his debt to Jeremy Bentham. He sounds very much like a Utilitarian when he praises Milton for his emancipation from "the servile worship of eminent men and the irrational dread of innovation" (*Works*, VII, 59). Remembering no doubt the Peterloo Massacre of 1819, which had shocked him as a Cambridge student, Macaulay writes in another essay that "the history of our country, since the peace of 1815, is almost entirely made up of the struggles of the lower orders against the government, and of the efforts of the government to keep them down."[4] He follows the Utilitarians by consistently taking a secular view of government in an age when appeals to religion were very common in politics. Macaulay separates politics from religion by attacking slavery on economic as well as moral grounds, and education from religion by arguing that the University of London should not be tied to the Church of England, as Oxford and Cambridge were (Clive and Pinney, pp. 7–11). He also urges that appeals to religion be kept out of scientific controversies ("Sadler's Law of Population," *Works*, VII, 584).

Unlike the Utilitarians, however, Macaulay was influenced by religion. His form of Utilitarianism has therefore been characterized as an "Evangelicalized Utilitarianism" in which "the Evangelical element made all the difference."[5] His support for reform and defense of oppressed minorities, for example, can be partly traced to his Evangelical background, although it is true that he rejected the doctrines of the Clapham Sect. What he retained was its fervor: the Methodists' emotionalism had been inherited by the Evangelicals, and as a result of his religious upbringing, Macaulay knew the importance of feelings. Thus in reviewing James Mill's *Essay on Government*, he attacks the Utilitarians for their insensitivity to emotion, as Dickens would later do in *Hard Times:* Mill and his followers "talk of power, happiness, misery, pain, pleasure, motives, objects of desire, as they talk of lines and numbers" (VII, 340). Macaulay's attack, based largely on common sense, forced John Stuart Mill to admit that his father's premises were too narrow, a crucial discovery for the younger Mill's intellectual development.[6] Finally, Macaulay differs from the Utilitarians in his strong attachment to an idea repugnant to them, "political trusteeship," that is, a belief that the upper and middle classes know what is best for the lower class. A direct connection between property ownership and political power is assumed.

Despite some fundamental differences of temperament and politics between Macaulay and the Utilitarians, he belongs with them in the broad category of those whose values were relative rather than absolute, secular rather than religious. A theme of "Machiavelli," for example, is the relativity of moral values: "Succeeding generations change the fashion of their morals, with the fashion of their hats and their coaches" (VII, 87). Macaulay argues that Machiavelli should therefore be judged not by the standards of a later time but by those of his own day. Assuming on the other hand that moral values are absolute and unchanging, James Anthony Froude attacked Macaulay in an essay titled "Reynard the Fox" for blurring the distinction between right and wrong when he wrote about Machiavelli.[7] But to a modern reader, the essay is stimulating precisely because it attempts to recreate the past without judging it.[8] The 1827 essay "Machiavelli" and Froude's response to it show the clash between a secular frame of reference and a religious one. Macaulay's essay is an early sign of the Victorian curiosity about process and development that tended to undermine the religious world view.

His interest in the circumstances that formed Machiavelli also shows his habit of seeing his topic in a new light, or taking an unexpected, sometimes paradoxical approach to a familiar subject. This habit, rather than any animus toward Plato, leads him to disparage Plato's philosophy in "Bacon." If others have portrayed Milton as a regicide and Machiavelli as a villain, Macaulay will show his inventiveness by taking new tacks. The importance of circumstances in these essays is clear not only from direct statements like those in "Machiavelli" about changing moral values, but also from the space Macaulay devotes to historical sketches in essays on one author, for example, passages describing the Puritans in "Milton," the condition of the eighteenth-century poet in "Samuel Johnson," and the changes in taste that led to Romanticism in "Byron."

The fact that they were originally written for the *Edinburgh*, edited by Francis Jeffrey (and later by Macvey Napier), accounts for other aspects of the essays. Jeffrey probably influenced Macaulay far more than has been recognized. Like Jeffrey, Macaulay tended to be a "trimmer."[9] He relied more on common sense than on theories and abhorred anything resembling mysticism. He also shared with Jeffrey and perhaps took from him the belief that circumstances rather than great men shape history. Both Jeffrey and Macaulay detested hero worship, and thus the word "authority" often bears unfavorable connotations in their writings. They took the authority of the reviewer very seriously, however, because they considered the judgment of books to be a public duty, especially important at a time when literacy was increasing. By occasionally calling a review a "tribunal," Macaulay refers to this judicial role. The didactic spirit of Jeffrey and Macaulay comes also from their belief that history furnishes a guide for the present. The reviewer could therefore shed light on current problems by examining them through historical parallels. The skill with which Macaulay finds and develops these is one impressive feature of his early reviews.

The cocksure tone of the reviews, thought peculiar to Macaulay, is in fact the usual tone of *Edinburgh* articles and reflects its motto: "Judex damnatur cum nocens absolvitur" (the judge is condemned when the guilty go free). One of the "guilty" was William Wordsworth, whose *Excursion* provoked a famous response from Jeffrey: "This will never do!" Like other reviewers, Macaulay freely abused authors; W. E. Gladstone alluded to the "scarifying and tomahawking power" which made him seem formidable.[10] He used the book being reviewed as a peg on which to hang his own ideas, a convention that tended to make the reviewer more important than the author. And, in a few cases, Macaulay's reviews, like Alexander Pope's *Dunciad*, secured fame for writers who would otherwise be forgotten.

Although Macaulay's authoritative tone was unremarkable for an *Edinburgh* contributor, his style seemed distinctive to Jeffrey: "The more I think, the less I can conceive where you picked up that style" (Trevelyan, I, 110). Balance and antithesis Macaulay could easily have picked up from eighteenth century prose or from Jeffrey himself, but Macaulay's language is more ornate and emphatic than Jeffrey's. A reason for this heightened language is suggested by a comment in one of Macaulay's letters: "It is not by his own taste, but by the taste of the fish, that the angler is determined in his choice of bait" (25 January 1830; Pinney, I, 261). Persuading the reader is equivalent to catching the fish. Since the early essays are chiefly argumentative, their stylistic devices should not be judged good or bad in themselves, but as effective or ineffective for argument.

The most noticeable rhetorical device in the early works, which accounts in part for their great length and results in part from Macaulay's fondness for citing historical parallels, is amplification. Contrasts, allusions, repetitions, and digressions are characteristic kinds of amplification in Macaulay. He will restate an idea figuratively after one or more of these methods have explained its literal meaning. He tends to see a thing not as it is in itself but in relation to something else. A related characteristic is that statements are seldom qualified. Ideas rapidly follow one another like beads on a string; little subordination develops within sentences. That is why Macaulay reads easily and why he occasionally seems shallow. To some extent his polemical end militates against careful qualifications, but his habit of explaining by paraphrase rather than by analysis weakens his argumentative works. When his starting point is an abstraction like government, as it is in "Southey" and the three essays on Utilitarianism, his devices of amplification sometimes obscure the issues. On the other hand, Macaulay treats concrete subjects very effectively. To illustrate this point, two early arguments will be examined, "Southey's Colloquies" and "Civil Disabilities of the Jews."

## II   *"Southey's Colloquies"*

When it appeared in 1829, *Colloquies on the Progress and Prospects of Society*, a series of conversations between Southey and the ghost of Sir Thomas More, was an obvious target for the *Edinburgh Review* because of its ultra-Tory sentiments and its attack on the industrial system. Macaulay's review became a famous declaration of Whig liberalism, although Southey's politics would today be identified as liberal.[11] Southey favors increased spending for public works and a strong paternal government, which Macaulay denounces as "meddling" and "all-devouring." His laissez-faire philosophy is stated most explicitly in the last two sentences of the review: "Our rulers will best promote the improvement of the nation by . . . leaving capital to find its most lucrative course, commodities their fair price, industry and intelligence their natural reward, idleness and folly their natural punishment. . . . Let the Government do this: the People will assuredly do the rest" (*Works*, VII, 502). Southey's paternal government is artificial, Macaulay implies here by repeating "natural"; but this strict laissez-faire doctrine seemed far less natural to later Victorian writers, as *Hard Times* and *Unto This Last* clearly demonstrate.

According to Macaulay, Southey discusses "trade, currency, Catholic emancipation, periodical literature, female nunneries, butchers, snuff, book-stalls and a hundred other subjects" (461), a catalogue that questions Southey's fitness to discuss politics and economics. Macaulay's strategy in the review is to pit common sense against his opponent's theories by distinguising between the right way to discuss government and a wrong way: government as a science versus government as an art. This statement is the thesis: "Government is to Mr. Southey one of the fine arts" (451). Thus Southey's method is labeled "picturesque" and "imaginative," while Macaulay's is "natural." Reiterated in direct statements and figurative paraphrases, the distinction between Macaulay's scientific reasoning and Southey's artistic perspective is the most important of the many sharp contrasts used to dismiss the opponent's case rather than to refute it. The art-science dialectic not only shapes the argument, in a sense it *is* the argument. Within its framework, since only Macaulay treats government scientifically, any of his facts can discredit Southey; and the questions the poet laureate has raised about the quality of life in an industrial age can be scorned as "imaginative."

John Holloway has shown that the favorable characterization an author makes for himself is an important argumentative strategy in Victorian prose.[12] Macaulay's assumption of a scientific, practical character in "Southey's Colloquies" is a good example. In "Byron," he notes that a fickle public has alternatively idolized and condemned the poet, adding, "We know no spectacle so ridiculous as the British public in one of its periodical fits of morality" (VII, 533). By implicitly contrasting his own impartial attitude toward Byron's life to the popular view, Macaulay characterizes himself as sensible and tolerant.

"Southey's Colloquies" has three main divisions. The introduction appraises Southey's earlier work, stressing his faulty method of treating politics. In the body, Macaulay considers Southey's views of the manufacturing system, political economy, and religion, and outlines the author's general view of the past. The conclusion argues that the false method that has led Southey into errors about the past (he has made "the picturesque the test of political good") naturally makes his view of the future wrong as well.

Macaulay's attitude toward Southey is one of high-spirited mockery rather than contempt, however. In the introduction, for example, he alludes to Southey's former radicalism and to *Paradise Lost*: "He has passed from one extreme of political opinion to another, as Satan in Milton went around the globe, contriving constantly to 'ride with darkness' . . . . It is not everybody who could have so dexterously avoided blundering on the daylight in the course of a journey to the antipodes" (459). Sallies of this kind often function in the argumentative essays to contrast the foolish, extremist author and the moderate reviewer. A less elaborate *argumentum ad hominem* than the one quoted here is the application of the term "sect" to the Utilitarians, to equate political unorthodoxy with religious. Macaulay's purpose in reviewing Mill's *Essay on Government* was less to evaluate Mill than to discredit the Utilitarians, because he feared the public would associate reform with radicalism. Utilitarianism, he concludes, "hurts the health less than hard drinking . . . and is immeasurably more humane than cock-fighting" (VII, 371).

In the sections on manufacturing and political economy, Macaulay celebrates the industrial growth which Southey had condemned. Today Southey's view seems prophetic, but it can be noted in Macaulay's defense that in 1830 the benefits of industrialism were far more obvious than their concomitant social evils. Macaulay accurately predicts that in 1930 machines will exist whose designs could not be imagined in 1830 (500). But he relies on narrow arguments against Southey, statistics on mortality for example, to deny that the manufacturing system harms workers. Southey had deplored the ugliness of the villages that sprang up when people left rural areas to work in factories. "Here are the principles on which nations are to be governed," Macaulay jeers in reply, "Rose-bushes and poor-rates, rather than steam-engines and independence" (466). A rather shadowy abstraction, "independence" is a logical consequence of steam engines, according to this sentence. The antithesis that opposes rose bushes to steam engines gives a concrete form to the art versus science dialectic upon which Macaulay's argument rests. The thesis that Southey views government as an art is reinforced by the claim that his opinions on finance will not appeal to "our hard-hearted and unimaginative generation." A descendant of the "unimaginative generation" whom Macaulay speaks for was Thomas Gradgrind, who told his pupils, "You must discard the word fancy altogether."[13]

Macaulay's arguments on wealth, which assume that the profit motive alone will create sufficient funds for public needs, rely mainly on a false analogy between the individual and the state. The state, for example, is called "one great capitalist" (498). Southey had distinguished between private spending and public. Macaulay accuses him of advocating an all-powerful state, "a Lady Bountiful in every parish, a Paul Pry in every house, spying, eavesdrop-

ping . . . spending our money for us, and choosing our opinions for
us" (475). Government here is obviously personified, a technique
that draws out the analogy between individual and state.

Turning to religion, Macaulay attacks the Tory belief that the
state should align itself with the church. Here the argument is more
effective because it does not rest on a simple contrast like art versus
science. Instead, Macaulay finds examples from history to extol religious liberty, as he had done in "Milton" and "Hallam." Since
powerful governments tend to be oppressive, from the Whig view-
point, history teaches that religious questions are best decided by
individuals. Not only an evil in itself, persecution wrongly extends
government power. The faith in "rugged individualism" seen earlier
in the review takes a more appealing form when Macaulay argues, in
the spirit of Milton's *Areopagitica*, that unrestricted discussion pro-
vides the best means of discovering truth. Here and in other works
Macaulay adds a practical argument: free speech is less dangerous to
the state than suppressed discontent. Another favorite point is that
the church is more likely to be corrupted by temporal power than to
be silenced by state opposition. Implying that he opposes only what
is bad for religion (a strong church-state union), Macaulay identifies
his position as the truly Christian one.

The three sections on manufacturing, economics, and religion are
followed by a description of Southey's "very gloomy" estimate of
social progress, one that rests on imagination rather than fact. But to
challenge Southey's belief that the English lower classes suffer great
hardships, Macaulay resorts to the imaginative method himself,
contrasting Englishmen to "the lazzaroni who sleep under the por-
ticoes of Naples [and] the beggars who besiege the convents of
Spain" (494). Starving Frenchmen in the early nineteenth century
were compelled to eat nettles and beanstalks, whereas the more
fortunate English lower class inhabits "the richest and most highly
civilized spot in the world" (496). Such reasoning reminds one why
economics was called "the dismal science." But Macaulay, to his
credit, later took a more humane view of the working class, as the
chapter on his speeches will show.

The conclusion of the review disputes Southey's pessimistic view
of the future of society. Unfortunately for Macaulay's literary reputation, his glowing account of progress has become a *locus classicus*
of Victorian optimism:

History is full of the signs of this natural progress of society. We see in almost every part of the annals of mankind how the industry of individuals, struggling up against wars, taxes, famines, conflagrations, mischievous prohibitions, and more mischievous protections, creates faster than governments can squander, and repairs whatever invaders can destroy. We see the wealth of nations increasing, and all the arts of life approaching nearer and nearer to perfection . . . .(499)

At first glance a rather vague synopsis, this passage reiterates specific arguments against Southey: the opposing phrases "industry of individuals" and "governments can squander" attack Southey's belief in the paternal state. The tax increase proposed by Southey is answered by joining taxes to such evils as war and famine. "Wealth is increasing" puts human suffering into a comforting perspective and refutes assertions that the condition of the working class is growing worse. Macaulay wishes the reader to believe that Southey's pessimistic view of the future results from blindness to the "signs of natural progress."

When passages such as the conclusion to "Southey" are taken out of context and reprinted in anthologies, their argumentative purpose cannot be understood. The amplified descriptions of progress here are intended to make Southey's pessimism seem foolish. Macaulay's purpose is only incidentally to urge an interpretation of history: as a reviewer for the leading Whig journal, he has a more immediate aim, to discredit the Tories. Proving Southey wrong about the future is a way of suggesting that Tory opposition to the Reform Bill is equally misguided.

The balanced sentences quoted above show Macaulay's trust in reason and order; they imply that we control our environment. Since Macaulay opposed his "natural" method of interpreting the past to Southey's "imaginative" method, he appropriately uses no contrived figurative language to describe progress but takes an image from nature: "A single breaker may recede; but the tide is evidently coming in" (500). The law of progress appears as fixed as the law governing tides.

The review of Southey's *Colloquies* encompasses a large area, the past progress of society and its probable destiny; but Macaulay's argumentative method obscures the complexity of these subjects. Nonetheless, his ideas are forcefully expressed, and the argument of

"Southey" is effective for a periodical work, one not meant to be reread and studied. An early argument that stands up better to analysis and demonstrates that Macaulay could be a far-seeing social critic as well as an apologist for the status quo is "Civil Disabilities of the Jews."

### III    "Civil Disabilities of the Jews"

Early in 1830, Macaulay wrote to Macvey Napier, who had succeeded Lord Jeffrey as *Edinburgh* editor: "The Jews are about to petition parliament for relief from the absurd restrictions which lie on them—the last relique of the old system of intolerance. I have been applied to by some . . . to write for them in the *Edinburgh Review*. I would gladly serve a cause so good—and you, I think, could have no objection" (25 January 1830; Pinney, I, 262). Jews at this time could not become judges or members of Parliament because of required oaths administered on the New Testament. One foundation of "Civil Disabilities of the Jews" is stated in this letter: Macaulay opposes not merely a single unjust law but "the old system of intolerance." The essay he wrote to elaborate this idea greatly influenced English public opinion: "it was regarded as the main statement of the Jewish case."[14]

"Civil Disabilities of the Jews" differs in some ways from other early works. It is much shorter (seventeen pages) than "Milton" or "Southey." It contains fewer exaggerations, elaborate paraphrases, and sharp contrasts than is usual in Macaulay, and more irony. But "Civil Disabilities of the Jews" characteristically stresses a moderate, practical approach to governing. As in other argumentative essays, liberty is an important theme.

Macaulay makes an appeal to Christian values an integral part of his argument against discriminatory laws. Whether this choice mirrors his personal belief is hard to know; probably it does not. But to say simply that he assumed a Christian posture for rhetorical effect would be misleading. Just as Macaulay in historical works projects himself imaginatively into the past, he summons up for this defense of the Jews a Christian zeal so crucial to his formation that he could express it unself-consciously throughout his life. Here the appeal to Christian morality serves a specific rhetorical function, however: it anticipates a common Tory charge that atheism lurks behind innovating legislation.

"Civil Disabilities of the Jews" is divided into four parts, corresponding to the four arguments Macaulay seeks to refute. First, the constitution of a Christian country will be destroyed if Jews are allowed to legislate; second, Jews are unpatriotic; third, since Jews expect a promised land, they are unconcerned about the welfare of England; fourth, full citizenship can be withheld from Jews because scripture predicts that they will be persecuted. As this list indicates, the essay begins with the strongest opposition claim and ends with the weakest. The framework into which the parts fit is suggested at the end of the introductory paragraph, when Macaulay denounces the present laws for maintaining a "system full of absurdity and injustice" (VIII, 1). "Absurdity" sums up the theories behind anti-Jewish legislation; "injustice" refers to their practical consequences.

In each part of the review, Macaulay attacks both the theory and the practice of Jewish disabilities. The phrase "in fact" marks transitions between these two aspects of the question. As an organizing principle, theory versus practice functions more effectively than the art versus science contrast underlying "Southey."

Macaulay finds three theoretical objections to the constitutional argument used to defend the status quo: civil disabilities produce no good to the community, only harm to the Jews; second, the right to own property, granted to Jews, carries with it a right to exercise political power because property can be protected only by this power; and third, since the fundamental ends of government are to maintain order and to protect property, religion has no bearing on a person's fitness to govern. After elaborating these ideas, Macaulay restates the point under debate to make it favor his position: "What is proposed is, not that Jews should legislate for a Christian community, but that a legislature composed of Christians and Jews should legislate for a community composed of Christians and Jews" (4). Since Christians differ as sharply among themselves on ecclesiastical questions as they differ from Jews (an exaggeration showing Macaulay's impatience with doctrinal disputes), Jews cannot logically be excluded from power because of their religious opinions.

In fact, Macaulay continues, Jews have the substance of political power in their wealth; therefore, discriminatory laws do not work. The first section concludes: "If it is our duty as Christians to exclude the Jews from political power, it must be our duty to treat them as our ancestors treated them, to murder them, and banish them, and rob them. For in that way, and in that way alone, can we really deprive them of political power" (6–7). Since murder and robbery are obviously not the duties of Christians, neither are less flagrant injustices. By listing the Jews' past sufferings, Macaulay implies that discriminatory laws maintain the old persecutions, a link that puts the opposition case in an unfavorable light.

The other three sections, though shorter than the first, also illustrate Macaulay's skill at imputing bad logic as well as bad Christianity to opponents of reforming legislation. His language becomes more scornful as he takes up the weaker anti-Jewish arguments.

The second part of the review answers the charge that Jews are unpatriotic and should therefore be denied legislative power. The rebuttal makes a circular argument of this claim: Jews are unpatriotic only because they have been mistreated, but rulers excuse mistreatment by citing Jews' lack of patriotism. The true order of cause and effect is obscured here because "foreign attachments are the fruit of domestic misrule" (8). Macaulay often chooses this metaphor to describe political processes. He calls the 1688 Revolution "the fruitful parent of reforms" (VIII, 444), for example, and condemns the first partition of Poland, which resulted from Frederic the Great's alliance with Russia, as "the fruitful parent of other great crimes" (IX, 639). To defend the Jews, he emphasizes the charge of misgovernment: "It has always been the trick of bigots to make their subjects miserable at home, and then to complain that they look for relief abroad; to divide society, and to wonder that it is not united . . ." (VIII, 8). This assertion shows Macaulay's vigorous phrasing ("trick of bigots") and the pattern of statement-paraphrase characteristic of his essays.

He further discredits the opposition by a homely analogy that makes its patriotism argument seem illogical: "If the Jews have not felt toward England like children, it is because she has treated them like a step-mother" (8). This is a more effective metaphorical thrust than the statement that Southey favors an "all-devouring" state; it draws an elucidating parallel to the actual situation, whereas the second example merely conveys Macaulay's dislike for Southey's opinion.

But, in fact, Jews are no less loyal than any excluded group, a point amplified through a hypothetical case that proves that discrimination is arbitrary: if all the red-haired people of Europe had been banished and tortured; if, "when manners became milder, they had still been subject to debasing restrictions . . . what would be the patriotism of the gentlemen with red hair?" (10). Following the rhetorical question is a short, ironical speech by a hypothetical opponent of full rights for the red-haired, who states that nature and experience prove red-haired men cannot be English citizens; "the constitution is . . . essentially dark-haired" (11). In this parody of opposition arguments, the reference to nature suggests that circumstances—not any innate qualities in them or in the constitution—have excluded the Jews from power. Only "milder manners" distinguish the persecutors of history from those who discriminate against Jews in 1831. The comparison to red-haired people is apt, too, because it implies that the Jews are a diverse group, a point Eliot makes in *Daniel Deronda* by portraying both a high-minded Zionist and a mercenary tradesman.

The third section of "Civil Disabilities of the Jews" refutes the argument that English Jews, desiring their own country, ignore the nation's welfare. Theoretically, this proposition is unsound because it demands reasoning from people's beliefs to their actions. Moreover, the argument ignores the fact that "what is remote and indefinite affects men far less than what is near and certain" (13). In theory, therefore, Jews can govern the community where they live even through they hope their children will be restored to the promised land. In practice, the fitness of Jews to legislate is guaranteed by the ordinary feelings they share with others, the wish to live peacefully and prosperously.

The final argument demonstrates most clearly that the present laws are both absurd and unjust: lawmakers will falsify scripture by giving full citizenship to Jews because scripture foretells that they will be homeless and persecuted. Macaulay protests that an act cannot be sanctioned merely because the Bible has predicted it: "If this argument justifies the laws now existing against the Jews, it justifies equally all the cruelties which have ever been committed against them, the sweeping edicts of banishment and confiscation, the dungeon, the rack, and the slow fire" (16). The most emphatic attack on a theory justifying persecution comes, appropriately, near the end of the essay. In practice, the scripture argument is foolish because Jews have full civil rights in France and the United States.

In a dramatic conclusion, Macaulay takes up a suggestion face-tiously made by the opposition that the bill removing Jewish dis-abilities be read on Good Friday: "We know of no day fitter for blotting out from the statute book the last traces of intolerance than the day on which the spirit of intolerance produced the foulest of all judicial murders, the day on which the list of the victims of intolerance, that noble list wherein Socrates and More are enrolled, was glorified by a yet greater and holier name" (16–17). Again Macaulay puts discriminatory laws into the larger context of persecution. Here he explicitly links the Jews to Christ. Joining the phrases "spirit of intolerance" to "judicial murder" suggests the same relationship between false theories and unjust acts that the introduction established by the words "absurdity" and "injustice."

While Macaulay's plea for the Jews seems unremarkable today, it was controversial at a time when the idea of the Christian state was so pervasive. Jews were barred from Parliament until 1858, twenty-eight years after "Civil Disabilities of the Jews" first appeared, and from other high offices until 1871. Macaulay's vigorous defense of Jewish rights was translated into six languages. A German translation was published in 1881, for example, in response to an anti-Semitic campaign.[15] And Macaulay's arguments were used in 1941 to attack Nazi persecution of the Jews.[16] The impact of "Civil Disabilities of the Jews" can also be measured by the fact that the *Quarterly Review* attacked it sixteen years after its appearance in the *Edinburgh*. The Tory writer claimed that the presence of Jews in Parliament would undermine Christianity and insisted that the "Christianizing of the State gives the greatest hope for the well-being of the people."[17] Macaulay had demolished this argument in 1831; for him, "the people" meant Jews as well as Christians.

Macaulay's vivid language sets his work apart from the work of other reviewers in the period 1825 to 1831. The concise essay on Jewish disabilities is more persuasive than "Southey," but both works are carefully structured and both show the argumentative uses of contrast, allusion, historical analogy, the hypothetical case, and metaphorical paraphrase. For a skillful handling of theoretical questions through these devices, one must turn to Macaulay's essay on Gladstone, but the earlier works, one a celebration of the age and the other a challenge to it, exemplify his polemical style.

### CHAPTER 3

# The Minute on Indian Education

## I  Background

IN one of his best parliamentary speeches, Macaulay supported a plan to reorganize the government of India by a compromise that limited the commercial power of the East India Company and provided that the country would be ruled by a Supreme Council (10 July 1833; *Works*, XI, 543–86). Members of the council, except for the legal member, would belong to the company. Parliament approved the plan, which also called for reform of the Indian penal code.

As the first legal member of the Supreme Council, Macaulay lived in India from 1834 to 1837. He went out expecting that his salary would make him financially independent for the rest of his life, an important consideration when he accepted the Indian appointment because his father, Zachary, had lost his fortune; and Macaulay, the eldest son, was the chief support of the family. He also thought of money because, as he said in a letter to his sister Hannah, he could not earn enough by writing to support himself while pursuing a career in politics. But when he returned from India, he could "act on all public questions without even a temptation to deviate from the strict line of duty" (17 August 1833; Pinney, II, 299; 301). Referring in the same letter to his "exile" (301), he begged Hannah to go to India with him, which she agreed to do. Macaulay suffered two great blows there, the marriage of Hannah to Charles Trevelyan and the death of his sister Margaret; he confided to his friend T. F. Ellis that reading classical literature saved him from a breakdown (8 February 1835; Pinney, III, 129).[1]

During the years that Indian affairs took up most of Macaulay's time, he wrote two long articles for the *Edinburgh Review*, "Bacon" and "Mackintosh"; and he planned a *History of England* that would

41

extend from the seventeenth century to the Reform Bill. Such an ambitious design would require that he make literature rather than politics his main occupation when he returned to England. Thus the Indian years were a turning point in his career.

His life and work in India are comprehensively described in the last four chapters of Clive's *Macaulay: the Shaping of the Historian*.[2] The Indian penal code, one of Macaulay's major accomplishments, reflects the same reforming zeal with which he treated the question of Jewish disabilities. He also played a key role in Indian education. When relatively few details were known about this role, it was thought that Macaulay single-handedly made English the language of instruction in India, by siding with Anglicists against Orientalists on the Committee of Public Instruction (Orientalists favored not the vernacular languages but Arabic and Sanskrit). As Clive's narrative convincingly demonstrates, however, the real story is far more complex and interesting. After tracing the history of the Orientalist-Anglicist controversy, Clive concludes that "much of the battle over English education had, in fact, been fought and won before Macaulay ever set foot in India."[3] But Macaulay's minute, enthusiastically championing English, became very influential.[4] A commentator on the Indian language riots of 1968 wrote that university students "would have been better advised to burn an effigy of Macaulay than to waste their energies in ordering shopkeepers to cover up all English language signs."[5]

The debate between Anglicists and Orientalists reflected differences that went beyond language: on opposing sides were "those who were looking ahead to a culture and people as far as possible assimilated to the West (and, more specifically, to Britain) and those who were looking ahead to an Indian culture and people revitalized by means of Western knowledge, but in their essence still Indian."[6] The program of the latter group was elitist in that only a few natives would acquire a knowledge of the ancient languages Arabic and Sanskrit.[7] Both sides approved the use of English, but sharply disagreed on the extent to which it should be taught.[8] Macaulay favored English, but not mass education. His compromise, which Clive terms "filtration," is expounded in the education minute: "It is impossible for us, with our limited means, to attempt to educate the body of the people. We must at present do our best to form a class who may be interpreters between us and the millions we govern." Macaulay's next words show his sense of racial superiority: the class through whom education would filter was to be "Indian in blood and color, but English in taste, in opinions, in morals, and in intellect" (Clive and Pinney, p. 249).

This same vision inspires the glowing conclusion of the 1833 speech: India can share in "the imperishable empire of our arts and our morals, our literature and our laws" (*Works,* XI, 586). This cultural empire is called "imperishable" to distinguish it from political power, which will be transitory, according to Macaulay, who seems to favor eventual self-rule for India. He clearly views dissemination of English as a means toward that end, for he believed strongly in the link between education and political liberty. Just as he defends education for the English against his contemporaries who feared that, having learned to read, the people would become readers of revolutionary tracts, Macaulay defends education for Indians against those who feared that British rule would be undermined by a literate native class: "I will never consent to keep [Indians] ignorant in order to keep them manageable, or to govern them in ignorance in order that we may govern them long," he declares in one of his last speeches.[9]

Since two of Macaulay's most eloquent parliamentary speeches concern India and education, it is not surprising that the topics are effectively combined in the minute. His views on education are hard to label because, on the one hand, he shared the radicals' faith in education and rejected the conservatives' argument that it would lead to anarchy; but in the 1830s the broad context for his ideas is laissez-faire liberalism.[10] Thus "Southey" is a good introduction to the minute on education because the review emphatically states a belief in laissez-faire that underlies the minute but is a much less prominent part of its argument.[11]

## II  *The Minute*

Before Macaulay arrived in India, Anglicists and Orientalists on the Committee of Public Instruction clashed on the interpretation of an 1813 Act of Parliament that directed that funds be used to encourage the study of Arabic and Sanskrit. In his capacity as legal member of the Supreme Council, Macaulay wrote a minute dated 2 February 1835, upholding the Anglicist position that money could be spent for English without violating the 1813 act. This minute, shorter than most of Macaulay's essays, can be divided into three parts. Macaulay first discusses the 1813 act as it bears on the controversy. He then gives his reasons for favoring English as the language of instruction. Finally, he refutes arguments for preferring Arabic and Sanskrit to English.

The Orientalists had said that a new law would be needed for English to supersede Arabic and Sanskrit, but Macaulay argues that although the 1813 act allocates funds for "reviving literature in India," it implicitly allows English by providing that money is also to be used to introduce scientific knowledge, which Macaulay takes to mean knowledge from the West. Moreover, the government had not promised always to support only Arabic and Sanskrit; a change would therefore not undermine public trust in the rulers of India. To defend his views, Macaulay cites analogous cases:

We commence the erection of a pier. Is it a violation of the public faith to stop the works, if we afterwards see reason to believe that the building will be useless? The rights of property are undoubtedly sacred. But nothing endangers those rights so much as the practice, now unhappily too common, of attributing them to things to which they do not belong [i.e., to grants for Arabic and Sanskrit]. Those who would impart to abuses the sanctity of property are in truth imparting to the institution of property the unpopularity and fragility of abuses. (Clive and Pinney, 239)

Similarly, in debates on reform, Macaulay had answered the Tories' claim that elimination of rotten boroughs took away private property by saying that Reform merely eliminated abuses that, if ignored, could lead to Revolution and the large-scale destruction of private property. Reform thus protected property.

Macaulay's analogy to government spending for a pier shows his fondness for concrete ways of treating issues, in this case the issue of Indian education. Here, as in the early essays, the advantage of the tactic—clarity—is offset to some extent by a disadvantage—oversimplification. When Macaulay ridicules discrimination against Jews by a hypothetical case of discrimination against people with red hair, his parallel is strikingly effective. But he sometimes equates the abstract or intangible with the physical. To express the thought that Scottish emigrants thrive all over the world, for example, he declares: "they rise above the mass of those with whom they mix, as surely as oil rises to the top of water . . ." (Works, VIII, 195).

A short paragraph joins the first part of the education minute to the second: "We come now the gist of the matter. We have a fund to be employed as Government shall direct for the intellectual improvement of the people of this country. The simple question is, what is the most useful way of employing it?" (Clive and Pinney, p. 240). The answers are sought, characteristically, from common sense and from lessons of the past. Anglicists and Orientalists agree that the vernacular languages are unsuited for the education of the natives, and both sides admit the superiority of Western languages to Arabic and Sanskrit. Since English will become increasingly important as the British Empire grows, English will be useful to Indians. Parallel cases from history lead to the same conclusion. Macaulay notes the importance of classical languages during the Renaissance: "What the Greek and Latin were to the contemporaries of More and Ascham, our tongue is to the people of India" (243). A second example is the civilizing influence of foreign languages upon Russia.

Macaulay's arguments in the second section of the minute can be viewed in two ways. On the one hand, the shrewdness of the rhetoric cannot fail to impress the reader. English for India will be good, as the rebirth of learning was good, as the influence of Western Europe upon Russia was good. To make a choice seem desirable, Aristotle recommended in the *Rhetoric*, compare it to whatever your audience accepts as good, a common strategy in Macaulay's arguments. At the same time, Macaulay's discussion of English is bound to seem chauvinistic to the modern reader. English is not merely praised as more useful to Indians but as "intrinsically superior" to Arabic and Sanskrit, a belief emphasized in several exaggerated statements. Clearly, the inferiority of these languages reflects the inferior quality of the learning conveyed by them, "medical doctrines which would disgrace an English Farrier— Astronomy, which would move laughter in girls at an English boarding school—History, abounding with kings thirty feet high, and reigns thirty thousand years long—and Geography, made up of seas of treacle and seas of butter" (242–43). This high-spirited recitation of errors shows the writer's insensitivity to cultures different from his own.[12]

In the last section of the minute, Macaulay refutes these arguments of the Orientalist party: only by encouraging the study of Sanskrit and Arabic will the English get cooperation from natives; these languages are sources for Hindu and Mahomedan law; they merit special treatment because of their sacred books; and the natives cannot master English. To answer the first of these objections to the policy he favors, Macaulay appeals to "the state of the market," that is, to the greater popularity of the ruler's language: Indians will pay to learn English but must be paid to learn Sanskrit and Arabic, a crucial distinction for a believer in laissez-faire. Macaulay cites complaints from students educated in Arabic and Sanskrit at government expense that they cannot support themselves and therefore view their education as an injury for which they should be compensated, a situation Macaulay finds ludicrous. "Surely," he protests, "men may be brought up to be burdens to the public . . . at a somewhat smaller charge to the state" (246). He also notes that the Committee of Public Instruction has been unable to sell works it has printed in Arabic and Sanskrit, while English books sell very well, another fact bound to impress the author of "Southey's Colloquies."

The other arguments of the Orientalists are quickly disposed of. The laws in Sanskrit will be superseded by the proposed penal code, a digest of Indian laws for which Macaulay was largely responsible.[13] As for religion, Macaulay thought the government should be neutral. If he expected good to come from the work of missionaries, he had more confidence in the civilizing influence of Christianity than in the truth of its doctrines. He states in the education minute, however, that to encourage the study of Sanskrit and Arabic for religious reasons would be to promote "monstrous superstitions" (248). He does not consider the literary importance of sacred works such as the *Vedas* or the related and even more significant question of cultural identity. But he argues that Indians are capable of mastering English, and his insistence on this point shows a respect for the subjugated race: he has heard natives discuss the education debate "with a liberality and an intelligence which would do credit to any member of the Committee of Public Instruction" (249), a statement that corresponds to his belief that natives should be entrusted with the highest public offices. The tone here may be patronizing, but Macaulay's attitude toward the people he helped to govern is not simply that of a superior toward inferiors. His assumption that the spread of English could strengthen Indian civilization has been taken to illustrate "the cosmopolitan spirit of the eighteenth century."[14]

A statement near the end of the minute expresses Macaulay's belief that "the state of the market" is relevant to the education debate. The people of India must be free to choose between "the rival systems of education" without British interference (250). Related passages call to mind a dichotomy underlying "Southey," that of natural versus artificial—laissez-faire doctrines representing the natural and paternal government the artificial. The minute recommends instruction in English as the natural course, retention of Arabic and Sanskrit as artificial. This is clear from Macaulay's allusion to "that oriental interest which we have, by artificial means, called into being" (247). Another statement suggesting the natural versus artificial dichotomy appears in the last paragraph of the minute: "I believe that the present system tends, not to accelerate the progress of truth, but to delay the natural death of expiring errors" (250). When English is adopted, in other words, the progress of truth will be accelerated and artificial means of instruction will be given up.

To distinguish so confidently between the natural and the artificial and to join the natural to the English language, Macaulay had to assume that the presence of the British in India was itself natural rather than artificial. To us it seems obvious that the natives' willingness to learn English was a survival tactic, that there could be no free competition among languages when one happened to be the language of the conquerors. The fact that a strategy for defending the Industrial Revolution against Southey is used later by Macaulay in an altogether different context, to urge the claims of English against Arabic and Sanskrit, suggests a certain inflexibility in his polemical method. Nonetheless, the education minute shows his talent for finding and elaborating arguments. It is more effective than "Southey's Colloquies" because it is more concise and concrete.

Macaulay's disparaging view of Indian culture in the minute should be seen in the context of more sympathetic attitudes expressed in speeches and legislative minutes. He warned his countrymen against making themselves a new caste in India, for example, because he did not wish English rule to become oppressive ("Government of India," *Works*, XI, 575). Unless a uniform system of justice is established, he declared, "We proclaim to the Indian people that there are two sorts of justice, a coarse one which we think good enough for them, and another of superior quality which we keep for ourselves."[15]

Macaulay's reforming spirit is also clear from his strong conviction that the Indians would eventually govern their own country. He viewed skeptically Gladstone's idea of a spiritual treaty, uniting the two countries, which justified English rule: "It is by coercion, it is by the sword, and not by free stipulation with the governed, that England rules India" ("Gladstone," *Works*, IX, 151). The truth of this blunt statement was proven by the Indian Mutiny of 1857. The killing of Europeans inflamed the English, whose vindictiveness alarmed Macaulay. He wrote in his journal that the outburst of vengeful feeling would harm the nation's character by weakening respect for life (17 September 1857; Trevelyan, II, 360). Macaulay wished to see a moderate, humane form of government for India. He frankly called it "despotism," but his faith in English institutions was strong enough to persuade him that it could be an "enlightened and paternal despotism" ("Government of India," *Works*, XI, 582). Disseminating the English language would be one way to prevent tyranny.

### CHAPTER 4

# "Gladstone on Church and State"

## I  Edinburgh *Essays 1831–1839*

IF the Reform Bill had not passed in 1832, Macaulay's reviews of the 1830s might have been as polemical as they had been in the 1820s. But his growing interest in history sufficiently explains the prominence of narrative works in the reviews written from 1831 to 1839. Only three essays in this period can be classified as arguments, but they are important for showing Macaulay's versatility: "Mirabeau" (1832), "Bacon" (1837), and "Gladstone" (1839). The narratives, all on English history, are: "Hampden" (1831), "Burleigh" (1832), "War of the Succession in Spain" (1833), "Horace Walpole" (1833), "The Earl of Chatham" (1834), "Mackintosh" (1835), and "Sir William Temple" (1838).

A comment Macaulay made to Napier about "Hampden" marks a transition from argumentative to narrative works: "It is in part a narrative. This is a sort of composition which I have never yet attempted" (9 January 1832; Pinney, II, 110). Although narrative passages can be found in earlier works, they serve an argumentative function, whereas narrative is clearly valued for its own sake in reviews written after 1831. A further distinction can be made between "survey narratives" of the 1830s that, though usually named after a person, are broad sketches of an age, and works of the following decade that focus more directly upon one man. When Macaulay refers to his "historical essays," he apparently means works of the latter category, which will be described in the following chapter.

Macaulay's contributions to the *Edinburgh* in the 1830s, especially the survey narratives, reflect some of the ideas and values that were later to shape the *History of England,* but the reviews are interesting in their own right. "Mackintosh," the work that most clearly foreshadows the *History* both in content and style, is also

49

memorable for a reason that will surprise those who consider book reviewing a thoroughly safe activity: William Wallace, editor of Mackintosh's *History of the Revolution in England in 1688*, was so enraged by Macaulay's attack upon him that he challenged him to a duel. The challenge, Macaulay coolly noted, was "very properly worded" (Trevelyan, I, 435). Luckily for the reviewer, who had never fired a gun, the dispute was settled by seconds, and the harshest of Macaulay's strictures were removed from the review when it was reprinted.

By contrast, the work of Sir James Mackintosh, a Whig historian with whom Macaulay sat in the House of Commons, receives very favorable treatment. Macaulay approves not only the author's judgments but also the liveliness of his narrative. Macaulay's interest in the art of historical writing is evident from this comment: "The triumph of [the historian's] skill is to select such parts as may produce the effect of the whole, to bring out strongly all the characteristic features, and to throw the light and shade in such a manner as may heighten the effect" (*Works*, VIII, 426). The first part of "Mackintosh" describes English history from the Restoration to the Revolution, 1660 to 1688. Macaulay then expatiates upon the "spirit and tendency" of the Revolution under two headings: changes in laws and changes in the public mind. Since both changes strengthened liberty, Macaulay praises the Revolution; but he is careful to qualify this praise, in a way uncharacteristic of earlier works, by noting that reforms were incomplete (490–91). The development of ideas in "Mackintosh" shows an improvement over earlier essays, and the narrative flows very smoothly.

In effect, "Mackintosh" looks forward to the later Macaulay. "Bacon," on the other hand, a review of more than one hundred pages, looks back to the florid prose of "Milton," to the method of arguing through sharp contrasts used in "Southey," and to the caricatures of "Samuel Johnson." The review is divided into two parts, Bacon's life and works, with three subjects in the second part: the end of Bacon's philosophy, as contrasted to that of ancient philosophy; his method; and his intellectual characteristics. His end is "fruit," practical good, as opposed to "thorns," a distinction that is amplified to the point where Macaulay seems to be attacking philosophy itself. But he notes with approval that Bacon was not a materialist, for "he was far too wise not to know how much our well-being depends on the regulation of our minds" (VIII, 619). And the same may be said for

Macaulay.[1] Although Bacon did not invent the method he used, induction, he gave it new importance, according to this essay. Bacon's mind appears remarkable to Macaulay because he excelled both at minute observation and at broad reasoning.

Often anthologized to represent Macaulay, "Bacon" shows only one of his many sides, his practical bent. Just as in other works he corrects false views—for example, the idea that private letters are unworthy of a historian's attention in "Temple"; and the idea that seventeenth century English politicians can be judged by nineteenth century standards of progress and reform in "Mackintosh"—in the Bacon essay he seeks to correct the view that philosophy has no practical ends. In taking the opposite view, Macaulay implies that philosophy should have only practical ends; but seen in the context of other arguments, the attack upon ancient philosophy can be interpreted as a means of emphasizing Bacon's importance. It is clear from Macaulay's admission to Napier that his essay was "very superficial in the philosophical part" that his primary aim was not to evaluate ancient thought.[2]

Macaulay's respect for Greek literature is demonstrated by his life-long habit of reading the classics and from observations in other works. In "Temple," for example, he says that reading Aristophanes enlarges the mind (IX, 20). An understanding of Macaulay's politics also helps to explain why Plato is disparaged and Bacon praised: Macaulay associates an acceptance of the status quo with pre-Baconian philosophy, while the philosophy that bears "fruit" by reducing human suffering is an ally of progressive, reformist politics. This distinction is implied rather than stated in "Bacon," but it is not surprising that Macaulay would see a philosophical question in political terms, since he occasionally uses a political frame of reference when considering a literary question. In the Bacon essay he speaks of ancient and scholastic philosophy as an "empire" and as "the fallen monarchy," and uses the words "revolution" and "anarchy" to describe the state of philosophy before Bacon.

In another argumentative work of the period, "Mirabeau," Macaulay defends the French Revolution. He had written in the Milton essay: "If men are to wait for liberty till they become wise and good in slavery, they may indeed wait forever" (VII, 43). In "Mirabeau" as in "Milton," he justifies rebellion by stressing the abuses of the system against which it was directed. Shifts of public opinion described in "Mackintosh" illustrate the action-reaction pattern Macaulay saw in history, and the same thought is presented in "Mirabeau": at the outset, the French Revolution inspired great hope; then its excesses and the resulting chaos made the revolution seem despicable; finally, the passing of time made its progressive character unquestionable. To understand a verdict on the revolution, therefore, one must know the circumstances at the time the judgment was made, i.e., whether abuses were more obvious than reforms. Thomas Carlyle's *French Revolution* (1837) tells what he felt about the event, while "Mirabeau" (1832) tells what Macaulay thought. Macaulay's interest lies in the political side of the revolution, Carlyle's in its human drama. The sense of mystery that pervades Carlyle's book is absent from Macaulay's essay. Since only three paragraphs at the end of the essay treat Honoré Mirabeau himself, it is difficult to compare Macaulay's view of the revolutionary leader with Carlyle's, but the distinction between flat characters and round seems apt: a few sentences in Carlyle bring a complex figure to life. Macaulay's broad generalizations and picturesque details are not well suited to character drawing.

Portraits in the essays of the 1830s show that high-spirited men appealed to Macaulay, who often ascribes "warmth" to them. In this group are John Hampden, Robert Walpole, William Pitt, and a hero of the Spanish war, the Earl of Peterborough. Among those Macaulay less readily identifies with, cold or cautious men, are William Burleigh, George Halifax, Horace Walpole, Francis Bacon, and William Temple. A willingness to break with tradition characterizes the men Macaulay admires. To emphasize Peterborough's skill, he contrasts him to a general "who thought it much more honorable to fail according to rule, than to succeed by innovation" (VIII, 296). Despite a belief that circumstances rather than heroes determine history, Macaulay likes to portray bold and colorful figures in action.

His success with "Hampden" (1831) is thus understandable, but a narrative written in 1838, "Temple," is superior to "Hampden," even though, as Macaulay admits, he felt no kinship with the seventeenth century diplomat and statesman (IX, 4). "Temple" is more complex than earlier survey narratives; political questions such as the Triple Alliance are thoughtfully discussed in the essay. More patient with theories than he had shown himself in "Bacon," Macaulay analyzes Temple's plan to make the Privy Council a check on the crown, in the light of the gradual shift of power from the crown to the House of Commons (IX, 60–76). The essay presents more specific information about Temple and the characteristics of his age than is given in "Hampden." Many events illustrate Temple's caution, giving the work a certain thematic unity. Transitions between Temple's public life and his periods of retirement are smoothly made. Temple is kept before the reader's attention, while historical sketches remain in the background. Finally, the ending shows a development in Macaulay's descriptive power, for earlier works end abruptly, whereas in "Temple" the conclusion comes gradually. Macaulay makes Temple's final retirement seem as interesting as his political life by recounting his part in the Ancients versus Moderns controversy, and by giving a few anecdotes about Temple's secretary, Jonathan Swift. "Little did Temple imagine that the coarse exterior of his dependent concealed a genius equally suited to politics and letters," a comment revealing Macaulay's eye for the improbable situations that make history interesting (IX, 96).[3]

## II   *"Gladstone on Church and State" (1839)*

Gladstone was a Liberal when he became prime minister in 1868, but he began his political career as a Tory, and his book *The State in its Relations with the Church* presents the strong defense of church establishment associated with high churchmen and the Tory party. Macaulay's opposition to the book centers on Gladstone's principles rather than on his belief in church establishment. Regarding the state as a spiritual entity, having a conscience like an individual's, Gladstone emphasizes its duty to teach the truth. Macaulay assails this justification for church establishment because for him the state is fundamentally secular. The basic disagreement between the writers reflects differing views of authority, Gladstone's readiness to accept authority and Macaulay's suspicion of it, a suspicion that leads him to espouse in "Gladstone," as in "Civil Disabilities of the Jews," complete civil and religious liberty for all English citizens. This stance seems reasonable today but was attacked in the Victorian period as indifference to religion. Macaulay anticipates such criticism by offering his own defense of church establishment.[4]

"Gladstone on Church and State," a work that deserves to be as well known as "Bacon and "Southey" but that has not often been anthologized, can be outlined as follows:

I Rebuttal to Gladstone's theory (*Works*, IX, 111–74).
  A The state should profess a religion.
    1 Propagating religious truth may be good in itself
      but is not an end of government.
    2 Gladstone's reasoning would justify attaching
      religion to many other combinations of people be-
      sides a state, eg., an army.
  B The state should establish a religion.
    1 Disproved by theory: a state that fulfills the
      proper ends of government is not necessarily suited
      to propagate true religion.
    2 Disproved by practice: most governments have been
      wrong on religious questions.
    3 Gladstone's argument against persecution, that the
      state cannot supervise religious opinion, applies
      equally to all forms of discrimination that he
      favors.
  C The established religion should be the Church of England.
    1 But this church has a very weak claim to apostolic
      succession, which Gladstone says it preserves.
    2 The church lacks the unity that Gladstone claims
      for it; diversity is one of its great strengths.
II Macaulay's theory of church-state relations (174–85).
  A Government should consider the religious education of
    the people a secondary end, though intrinsically more
    important than maintaining order and protecting property.
  B Consequences.
    1 All discriminatory laws are indefensible and make
      government less efficient for its primary ends.
    2 No government should threaten order by forcing re-
      ligious instruction on the people.
    3 The religion of the majority generally should be
      taught.
    4 The Anglican church should be preserved: with all
      its faults it is better than what would replace it.
    5 National churches maintained by force (Ireland) are
      wrong; under them, both spiritual and temporal
      interests suffer.

The outline indicates an obvious difference between "Southey" and "Gladstone": in the later work Macaulay more fully and directly offers alternatives to the theories he has questioned.

If Macaulay's essays reveal no growth or development, as both nineteenth and twentieth century critics have claimed, the 1839 essay "Gladstone on Church and State" should closely resemble "Southey's Colloquies," since both are arguments treating some of the same political questions from the same Whig point of view. But the essays are quite different. The political stance of "Gladstone" is less conservative than that of "Southey"; its tone is better suited to argument; and, in general, "Gladstone" is more complex than earlier arguments. The last characteristic is especially apparent in Macaulay's use of antithesis and metaphor.

Implicit in early works, notably "Southey," is the assumption that laissez-faire is a sound principle in spheres other than economics; thus Macaulay takes the position that whatever people can do for themselves, the state is unlikely to do better for them. In "Gladstone," however, he acknowledges a more complex relationship between individuals and the state by distinguishing the main ends of government from such secondary ends as support for art and promotion of scientific research. Although government is not established for these purposes, it "may have at its command resources which will enable it, without any injury to its main end, to pursue these collateral ends far more effectually than any individual or any voluntary association could do. If so, government ought to pursue these collateral ends" (176). The key words here—"far more effectually than any individual"—mark a change from the narrow laissez-faire attitude of "Southey," in which Macaulay argued that public money should not even be used to build railroads. He later changed his mind ("The Ten Hours Bill," 22 May 1846; Clive and Pinney, p. 196). G. M. Young considers Macaulay's change of opinion remarkable because the railroads were "the triumph of private enterprise."[5] The rationale for strong government implied in the Gladstone passage is more explicit in parliamentary speeches of the 1840s in which Macaulay questions the broad application of laissez-faire. He declares, for example, that free competition is not necessarily good in education simply because it is good in trade; to link education to trade requires a false analogy ("Education," 19 April 1847; *Ibid.*, p. 220).

This stand indicates a modification of Macaulay's Whig philosophy, not a fundamental change in it. His political judgments became more pragmatic as he grew older, a result perhaps of his experience in India. In "Gladstone" he does not sharply oppose private independence and state power but opposes instead his view of the uses of power to Gladstone's, a less abstract distinction. Unfortunately for Macaulay's literary reputation, the ideas of the Southey review, "a Victorian glorification of self-help,"[6] are much better known than the political opinions of "Gladstone."

But "Gladstone" represents Macaulay equally well; and, because of its restrained tone, the essay exemplifies his best argumentative manner. The opening paragraphs establish the tone. Writing a thoughtful book is a particularly impressive feat for a House of Commons orator, Macaulay says in praise of his opponent, because a politician can speak and lead effectively without being profound. Thus "the tendency of institutions like those of England is to encourage readiness in public men, at the expense of fulness and of exactness" (*Works*, IX, 113). This stricture is interesting not only because it is seldom recognized that Macaulay could speak candidly of weaknesses in British institutions but also because his own parliamentary speeches were compared to Burke's. The qualification at the beginning of the statement, "the *tendency* of institutions," would be out of place in an early argument like "Southey."

The tone of "Gladstone" is well illustrated by a transitional comment that follows the rebuttal section: "Perhaps it would be safest for us to stop here. It is much easier to pull down than to build up" (174). That this was not merely ceremonial politeness is shown by a letter to Napier in which Macaulay says that although he could refute Gladstone's theories, he had difficulty finding "a good counter theory." He adds, "I catch only glimpses here and there of what I take to be the truth" (26 February 1839; Pinney, III, 277). This caution differs greatly from the youthful exuberance that marks Macaulay's bludgeoning assaults on Thomas Croker, Robert Montgomery, and Robert Southey. In the intervening years, Macaulay had been bitterly attacked in the Calcutta press, an experience that may have tempered his own attacks. Or he may have treated Gladstone judiciously because of his wide knowledge of religious controversy and church history.

In any case, Macaulay treated his opponent with marked courtesy, perhaps because he had a genuine liking for him. In a letter to his sister Selina, Macaulay describes Gladstone as "an excellent fellow: good-natured, honest, industrious, and well-read" (18 February 1839; Pinney, III, 276). A few weeks later he tells his sister

Hannah that not a single line of his essay on Gladstone could be judged "at all indecorous" (20 March 1839; Pinney, III, 280). Gladstone must have agreed, for he sent Macaulay a letter of thanks. "In these lacerating times," he wrote, "one clings to everything of personal kindness in the past" (10 April 1839; Trevelyan, II, 5), and Macaulay replied politely. This exchange of letters and the review itself help to correct the exaggerated portrait of Macaulay as the scourge of all Tories.

A third sign of a more flexible argumentative method in "Gladstone," besides its political stance and restrained tone, is that antithetical patterns are less rigid than those of earlier arguments. When Macaulay writes, for example, that Gladstone's rhetoric, "though often good of its kind, darkens and perplexes the logic which it should illustrate" (*Works*, IX, 114), he avoids rigidity by balancing two words with one (darkens, perplexes/illustrates) and by inserting the phrase "often good of its kind" to qualify the adverse judgment. Artificial by comparison are the sharp distinctions between art and science posed by "Southey" and between good and bad philosophy in "Bacon."

Two important functions of antithesis in "Gladstone" are to reinforce a key distinction in the essay and to summarize individual points, often in terse phrases or sentences. In this essay, as in "Civil Disabilities of the Jews," Macaulay contrasts what he judges a misapplication of Christian teaching to his own, sounder position. He creates the impression that his debate with Gladstone pits a traditionalist (himself) against an innovator; he wishes to appear a more orthodox and trustworthy defender of religion than Gladstone himself. Thus he carefully notes in beginning his challenge to Gladstone, whom he describes as "the rising hope" of the "stern and unbending Tories" (111), that an attack on Gladstone's view of church-state relations is not necessarily an attack upon church establishment per se. And since his differences from Gladstone are portrayed as relative rather than absolute, the author versus reviewer antithesis need not be overworked; it is only one argumentative strategy.

The traditionalist-innovator dialectic appears when Macaulay links Gladstone to the Tractarians, an effective way of imputing extremism to him. Others must have found the connection plausible, because Gladstone later recalled that in the early 1840s, "although I had little of direct connection with Oxford and its teachers,

I was regarded in common fame as tarred with their brush."[7] By connecting Gladstone to Oxford and thereby appealing to the British distrust of theories, Macaulay anticipates Kingsley's attempt, in a more famous Victorian religious debate, to distinguish his common sense from Newman's extreme subtlety, although Kingsley proved far less skillful at argument than Macaulay. Macaulay's suspicion of Tractarians is clear not only from "Gladstone" but from this plea in a speech on the sugar duties: "Let us at least keep the debates of this house free from the sophistry of Tract Number Ninety" (*Works*, XII, 114), a reference to Newman's claim that the Thirty-nine Articles bear a Catholic interpretation.

Macaulay says that Gladstone's view of private judgment counters the traditional Protestant teaching: "The Romanist produces repose by means of stupefaction. The Protestant encourages activity, though he knows that where there is much activity there will be some aberration. Mr. Gladstone wishes for the unity of the fifteenth century with the active and searching spirit of the sixteenth" (IX, 157). Macaulay hints that Gladstone's theory is only half Protestant, at the same time establishing his own trustworthiness by a harsh description of Catholicism. The negative connotations of "Romanist" make it more forceful here than the neutral "Roman Catholic." The antithesis of the last sentence, unity-active and searching spirit, lacks the exact balance that makes antitheses in earlier arguments seem mechanical. Unity in itself is not objectionable, only the unity resulting from "stupefaction." The strategy behind the juxtaposition of unity to active and searching spirit resembles a strategy in the *Areopagitica:* Milton condemns restrictions on liberty by comparing them to "Romish" tactics. The Catholic taint Macaulay professes to find in Gladstone's interpretations of apostolic succession and private judgment probably reflects his Evangelical upbringing.

He also chooses antithetical patterns to give force to his summaries. To dispute Gladstone's view that dissenters should be excluded from public office, for example, he argues that the policy fosters hypocrisy: "It is very much easier to find arguments for the divine authority of the Gospel than for the divine authority of the Koran. But it is just as easy to bribe or rack a Jew into Mahometanism as into Christianity" (137). The link implied here between force and error illustrates a premise of the essay—the arbitrary nature of state intervention in religious questions. The epigrammatic quality of Macaulay's summaries is shown by the comment that "it is just as easy to bribe or rack a Jew into Mahomatanism as into Christianity." If the criterion of truth makes the Gospel and the Koran antithetical, force can make them allies. Macaulay repeats another point from "Civil Disabilities of the Jews": torture and discriminatory laws result from the same intolerant spirit.

In the section of the rebuttal dealing specifically with the Anglican church, Macaulay answers Gladstone's claim that unity is one of its distinguishing marks by citing many examples of disunity. He then asks: "Is it not mere mockery to attach so much importance to unity in form and name, where there is so little in substance, to shudder at the thought to two churches in alliance with one state, and to endure with patience the spectacle of a hundred sects battling within one church?" (171).

Despite its exaggeration, the rhetorical question is effective because at the time Macaulay wrote, only a few years before Newman's conversion, conflicts within the Anglican church were very deep, rivaling older hostilities between churchmen and dissenters. Thus Macaulay's antithetical sentences seem more natural than many in "Southey." Although it suits Gladstone's argumentative purpose to stress unity in the church and Macaulay's to stress diversity, opposing viewpoints here also indicate a temperamental difference between the Tory writer and the Whig, the former preferring order to freedom when the two clash, and the latter believing freedom to be the more important.

But Macaulay believes the Anglican church should be maintained in England because "she teaches more truth with less alloy of error than would be taught by those who, if she were swept away, would occupy the vacant space" (182). The phrase "more truth with less alloy of error" succinctly defines a moderate position: if the church embodied pure truth, Gladstone's belief that it should be a more dominant power in the state might be justified; if the church were entirely corrupt, Macaulay might sympathize with the radicals' wish to destroy it. Another effective summary is the observation regarding the Anglican church that "her frontier sects are much more remote from each other, than one frontier is from the Church of Rome, or the other from the Church of Geneva" (182). The idea of ideological difference is made concrete by the comparison to physical distance. Antithesis in these examples leads not as in "Southey" and "Bacon" to two sharply distinct parts, but to a more complex structure, consisting of three terms which shape the mean between extremes:

extreme (radical)    mean (Macaulay)    extreme (Tory)

The argument ends with the following antithetical statements which also recommend compromise: "The world is full of institutions which, though they never ought to have been set up, yet, having been set up, ought not to be rudely pulled down . . . it is often wise in practice to be content with the mitigation of an abuse which, looking at it in the abstract, we might feel impatient to destroy" (184–85). Here the effect of antithesis is discrimination rather than over simplification. Macaulay admits the appeal of radical change, while at the same time arguing against it.

Through summary antitheses like the one that concludes the review—"it is often wise in practice to be content with the mitigation of an abuse which . . . we might feel impatient to destroy"— Macaulay says in a few words what would have been greatly amplified in an earlier essay. Commonplaces in "Gladstone" are tersely phrased—"it is easier to tear down than to build up"— whereas in "Southey" they are lengthily elaborated, often through loose metaphorical paraphrases that emphasize without refining the original expression. Metaphor in the Gladstone essay is more functional.

Macaulay does not rely heavily on metaphor to attack either Southey or Gladstone; profusion of metaphor is not characteristic of his argumentative prose, as it is of Carlyle's. Nonetheless, metaphors in the 1839 work reveal a development in Macaulay's style for, like summaries cast in antithetical form, they sharpen the argument without oversimplifying it. Value judgments simplified through metaphors of natural process, for example, the idea that material progress is inevitable expressed in this line, "a single breaker may recede; but the tide is evidently coming in" (Southey," VII, 500), are absent from "Gladstone," as are figurative expressions that elaborate sharp contrasts, for example, the "creeping snake" that stands for Bacon's life, and the "soaring angel" that represents his writing. Metaphors in "Gladstone" are more suggestive, as the following examples will illustrate.

Macaulay claims his opponent's arguments against persecution of dissenters are either invalid or can be used against him: Gladstone's "artillery" is of two kinds, "pieces which will not go off at all, and pieces which go off with a vengeance, and recoil with most crushing effect upon himself" (IX, 141). That is, if government is unable to investigate citizens' beliefs, as Gladstone admits when arguing against persecution, then the discriminatory laws he supports are unjustified on the same grounds. The idea of negative evidence is vividly expressed in the image of a recoiling cannon. Moreover, the allusion to firearms obliquely hints at a charge made earlier, that minorities may react violently to state-imposed religion.

Macaulay defends the decision of William the Third to allow Scotland a separate church: the union of England and Scotland, one nation but two churches, "resembles the union of the limbs of one . healthful and vigorous body, all moved by one will, all cooperating for common ends" (154). Gladstone therefore, the comparison implies, opposes what is natural and what works well in practice. Macaulay argues from consequences that the tranquil state of Scotland, compared to Ireland, disproves Gladstone's theory that church and state should be closely joined. Through the body metaphor and the Scotland-Ireland example, Macaulay distinguishes mistaken author from sensible reviewer more subtly than in "Southey's Colloquies." The image of the mutually dependent parts of a body (England and Scotland) "cooperating for common ends" embodies Macaulay's theme that people need not agree on religion to live together harmoniously. In this essay Macaulay proves, according to Hippolyte Taine, that the state "is only a secular association, that its end is wholly temporal . . . that in entrusting to it the defense of spiritual interests, we overturn the order of things."[8] Macaulay chooses a familiar metaphor for political harmony, which Shakespeare used in the opening scene of *Coriolanus:* Menenius applies the fable of the belly to the "mutinous members" of the Roman body, the plebeians, to persuade them that rebellion will harm their own interests.

Another apt metaphor resolves the problem of government grants to dissenters. Macaulay notes that differences among Anglicans are so pronounced that grants to churchmen, as well as to dissenters, may be used to teach various and conflicting doctrines. The question is one of degree; statesmen must be guided by circumstances. Then he summarizes: "That tares are mixed with the wheat is matter of regret; but it is better that wheat and tares should grow together than that the promise of the year should be blighted" (172). The reference (Matthew, 13: 29–30) is to the householder's command that wheat and tares in his field be allowed to grow together until the harvest. By alluding to this parable, Macaulay suggests that members of different religions should be equal in the state, as the wheat and the tares are equal until the harvest; and he implicitly links Gladstone to the men in the story who wish to burn the tares but are restrained by their master.

The parable sums up Macaulay's whole argument. It praises in a concrete way the abstract ideal of religious toleration. Between Tory and radical extremes—strengthening the established church and abolishing it—lies the moderate course of gradual reform. Such a compromise may be theoretically objectionable, just as allowing the tares to stay with the wheat may seem objectionable, but it offers practical advantages.

Macaulay's use of Bible language is telling for several reasons: through the parable he stresses his orthodoxy while challenging Gladstone's, acknowledges the importance of spiritual questions, and reinforces his argument that too close a church-state union can be detrimental to both institutions. In "Southey" he openly denounces Tory beliefs, but in this review he is more subtle, using metaphors to attack the opposition.

The Bible language in "Gladstone," used paradoxically to urge a secular view against a religious one, links Macaulay to other major Victorian prose writers, including Carlyle and Eliot, who lost their faith but did not cast off the language of their intensely religious childhoods. Victorian intellectual life was marked not only by clashes between a religious spirit and a secular spirit but also by their union. Thomas Huxley's debate with Bishop Wilberforce on evolution is an example of the clash, while Eliot's novels and Macaulay's argumentative essays show how the religious can be interwoven with the secular.

Although the laissez-faire principles that a cocksure Macaulay expounded in 1830 are considerably softened by 1839, the defense of religious liberty is just as vigorous in "Gladstone" as in the essays on Milton (1825) and Hallam (1828). Macaulay's objections to church-state alliances based on government leaders' ideas of truth are summarized near the end of the review by an attack on an institution defended by Gladstone, the Church of Ireland, which Macaulay describes as "a church established and maintained by the sword, a church producing twice as many riots as conversions . . .

possessing great wealth [and] long backed by persecuting laws . . ." (183). Macaulay's sympathy for oppressed Catholics is clear.

Curiously, a declaration very much like this one was written by Gladstone in 1868, when he was a Liberal who favored disestablishment of the Irish church. In the course of defending his changed position, he looks back on Macaulay's analysis of his book and admits that Macaulay's view of church-state relations has been vindicated. But he still believes that Macaulay separated too sharply the civil and religious duties of the state. To justify his earlier view of church and state, Gladstone cites the circumstances of the time, as Macaulay often does. In the 1830s, he recalls, the Anglican church experienced a great revival; piety and zeal were no longer regarded suspiciously. Thus it was easy for a young man like Gladstone "to form an over-sanguine estimate of the probable progress of the church in her warfare with sin and ignorance."[9]

Macaulay's own youthful warfare with ignorance was conducted in the pages of the *Edinburgh Review*. His early debates with his contemporaries bear the marks of intemperance and rashness, a nineteenth century French critic wrote, but as he grew older "les attaques, très vive encores, se sont modérées . . . le ton est devenu moins agressif."[10] The essay on Gladstone, Macaulay's last argumentative work, is the best example of his "less aggressive" style. Argumentative passages appear in later reviews, but these works are primarily narratives, reflecting a growing preoccupation with historical subjects. Thus, far from being all of a piece, the essays show a movement away from polemical to descriptive writing. Moreover, the polemical works show changes that "Gladstone," a more restrained and complex argument than "Southey," amply illustrates.

### CHAPTER 5

# *"Lord Clive"*

## I  Edinburgh *Essays 1840–1844*

IN the decade following his return from India, Macaulay's versatility was even more apparent than it had been before. He was elected to Parliament from Edinburgh and made secretary at war in 1839. In 1842, his popular poems the *Lays of Ancient Rome* were published. *Critical and Historical Essays Contributed to the Edinburgh Review*,[1] which appeared in the next year, became one of the most widely read works of the Victorian period. Macaulay attained another cabinet post in 1846, paymaster general, but was defeated in the election of 1847.[2] With the publication of the first two volumes of the *History of England* in 1848, Macaulay assumed the role most important to him. A few years earlier he had written to Macvey Napier, the *Edinburgh* editor, "I will not found my pretensions to the rank of a classic on my reviews" (24 June 1842; Trevelyan, II, 59). But the historian did not overshadow the essayist.

By the 1840s, however, Macaulay wished to confine his periodical writing to subjects related to the *History*. And in 1844 he wrote his last *Edinburgh* essay, "The Earl of Chatham," a continuation of an earlier work on the eighteenth century statesman. Other historical essays in this period are "Lord Clive" (1840), "Warren Hastings," (1841), and "Frederic the Great" (1842), three of Macaulay's best known short works. The survey narratives, those that have no hero as a focal point, are "Ranke's History of the Popes" (1840), "Comic Dramatists of the Restoration" (1841), and "Barère" (1844), which treats the French Revolution and is in part a philippic, with a leader of the Committee of Public Safety, Barère, as its target. A panegyric on a good friend, "Lord Holland" (1841), differs from other *Edinburgh* essays in being short and rather personal, but its sketches of the Fox family resemble historical passages in Macaulay's other reviews.[3] Finally, there are two articles published in 1843 that anticipate the *Encyclopaedia* essays of the next decade, for they skillfully blend literary criticism and biography: "Madame D'Arblay" (Fanny Burney) and "Addison." These works, which support Macaulay's contention that his last *Edinburgh* essays are better than his early ones (Trevelyan, II, 74), and which therefore deserve to be better known, will be discussed in the next chapter.

Macaulay's great interest in the survival of institutions, illustrated throughout Hamburger's *Macaulay and the Whig Tradition*, would have led him to study the work of the German historian Leopold von Ranke, *The Ecclesiastical and Political History of the Popes of Rome during the Sixteenth and Seventeenth Centuries*. But he had a more specific reason as well: struggles between Roman Catholics and Protestants were important in the period recreated by the *History of England*. The review "von Ranke" is best remembered for a passage in which Macaulay suggests that the Catholic church may outlive the British Empire: he imagines a traveler from New Zealand seeing the ruins of London Bridge and St. Paul's (*Works*, IX, 288). In a letter written to his father when he was fifteen, he quotes a paragraph from Jean Sismondi that is apparently the source of the famous New Zealander passage (14 May 1816; Pinney, I, 78–79).

To explain why Catholicism did not disappear after the Reformation, Macaulay argues that theology is not a progressive science (*Works*, IX, 288–94), an interesting clarification of his idea of progress. But he does not explain why the work of Ranke is important. Most of the review is devoted to analyzing four movements that threatened Rome: (1) the Albigensian heresy, a form of dualism that led to the Inquisition; (2) the Great Western Schism of the fourteenth century, which developed when rival popes sat at Rome and Avignon; (3) the Reformation, described in a long section; and (4) the scepticism of Voltaire and the French Revolution. An institution capable of sustaining these vicissitudes and showing signs of a nineteenth century revival wins Macaulay's "reluctant admiration" (317).

But despite his freedom from the anti-Catholic prejudices of his age and despite the popularity of the essay among Catholics, Macaulay is no apologist for Rome. "Among the contrivances which have been devised for deceiving and oppressing mankind," he pointedly declares, the Catholic church ranks first (316). But its political craft and its survival were bound to impress him, and by treating these in a neutral spirit he offended some readers. James Stephen, grandfather of Virginia Woolf, complained to Napier that he was "a little unhappy that there should be exultation in Rome (for such I hear is the fact) over a paper published in the city of John Knox, by a member of the British Cabinet."[4]

A more characteristic Victorian attitude than reluctant admiration for the Catholic church, and one more likely to cause exultation in Bloomsbury than in Rome, appears in "Comic Dramatists of the Restoration": Macaulay considers the plays immoral and a "disgrace" to the nation. Adultery is represented not as a vice, he complains, but as "the calling of a fine gentleman" (IX, 341). It should be noted, however, that Macaulay is offended as much by the "singularly inhuman spirit" of Restoration plays as by their immorality, and that he finds a cause of and partial justification for these excesses in a reaction to Puritanism. His stress on circumstances is shown by the connection he makes between the Puritans and the playwrights. Moreover, he strongly defends publication of the plays both because reading literature is a good in itself and because it illuminates a past age. "The virtue which the world wants is a healthful virtue . . . which can expose itself to the risks inseparable from all spirited exertion," Macaulay writes to defend the reading of Restoration drama.[5]

The review contains lively sketches of William Wycherley, William Congreve, and Jeremy Collier. The parable of the wheat and the tares used in "Gladstone" reappears in this work to argue that the state, controlled in this case by the Puritans, should not meddle in religion. Macaulay adds: "To know whether a man was really godly was impossible. But it was easy to know whether he had a plain dress, lank hair, no starch in his linens, no gay furniture in his house; whether he talked through his nose, and showed the whites of his eyes; whether he named his children Assurance, Tribulation, and Maher-shalal-hash-baz . . ." (350). Thus the Puritans, like the Restoration dramatists, went to extremes.

Attacks on religious intolerance and censorship in "Comic Dramatists of the Restoration" are manifestations of the liberty theme that is prominent in the *Edinburgh* works of 1840 through 1844. In "Warren Hastings," Macaulay does not hesitate to use the terms "atrocities" and "crimes" to describe some British acts in India. Burke is praised in this article for siding with America during the revolutionary war and for eloquently describing victims of

British misrule in India. Oppression of a different sort is indirectly attacked in a vivid sketch of the Reign of Terror that is often excerpted from "Barère." And Macaulay praises Frederic the Great for granting freedom of speech to his Prussian subjects.

The article on Frederic colorfully relates his military exploits, but Macaulay, unlike Carlyle, has ambivalent feelings toward them: he describes the devastation of Prussia resulting from the Seven Years War and observes that one-sixth of Prussia's male population died on the battlefield. The political administration of Frederic interests Macaulay as much as his military prowess. Sketches of Voltaire's adventures at Frederic's court and Frederic's treatment of Voltaire, somewhat fuller than sketches in earlier essays and less dependent on sharp contrasts for characterization, convey the same high-spirited satirical humor as the letters on parliamentary figures and events that Macaulay wrote to his sisters.

More complex narratives than "Frederic the Great" treat the eighteenth century English figures Hastings and Pitt the elder. The first governor general of India, Hastings was impeached when he returned to England, a circumstance that gives Macaulay's essay a special relevance in the 1970s, although its accounts of political intrigue, personality clashes, and colonial exploitation have perhaps never lost their relevance. Impeachment, says Macaulay, is "a fine ceremony" but not a useful one because it is too slow and too political (IX, 533). The essay has two sections, Hastings' Indian career and his later life in England, of which the most striking part is the description of his trial. Hastings is seen as an essentially good and public-spirited man but one guilty of crimes and bad judgment. A strength of the essay is Macaulay's attempt to interpret English actions in India as they would have been felt by the natives. And when one of Hastings' enemies escapes from prison by sliding down a rope made of his followers' turbans, we are clearly meant to admire his daring. Macaulay's longest essay except for the essay on Bacon, "Hastings" shows a skillful combination of analysis and narrative.

An even better illustration of this skill is "The Earl of Chatham," Macaulay's last periodical essay and his second devoted to Pitt. Written in 1834 and 1844, respectively, the two essays show Macaulay's development, for the first is a hasty sketch, while the second is a carefully constructed narrative that was revised three times.[6] Displaying a great knowledge of English history and politics, the second essay differs from the first in its characterization and use of dramatic techniques. Pitt is more fully delineated in 1844: his feelings, motives, domestic life, illnesses, the attitudes of others toward him, and the values implicit in his speeches are all described. Scenes replace the summary passages of 1834. The theme of a great man's fall, foreshadowed in a scene describing the 1762 session of Parliament and by the fall of Newcastle, is most dramatically presented in the last scene: Pitt attacks the proposed treaty between England and America and suffers an apoplectic fit. Ironically, he sides against the public good after having been an opponent of the war, but the cause of this reversal is his "distempered mind." In a somber tone, Macaulay describes Pitt's last, tragic appearance in Parliament and his funeral. The quiet solemnity at the end of this essay shows a side of Macaulay not seen in anthology selections. Yet the essay on Pitt, a mature work, represents the writer as well as a youthful composition like "Southey."

## II  *The Historical Essay*

The best example of Macaulay's narrative art among the last *Edinburgh* essays is "Lord Clive," one of his most famous works, which, like "Warren Hastings,"," is set in India. Macaulay's conception of the historical essay sheds considerable light on his practice in the Clive essay. Although he wrote no commentary on the historical essay as a distinctive genre, his theory of it can be gleaned from general comments on the art of historical writing and from specific references to his own works in his letters.

The view of history he expounded in an 1828 article will be discussed in Chapter 8. For the historical essay, the relevance of the article lies in parallels drawn between history and other arts: biography, fiction, drama, and painting. Macaulay cites Boswell's *Life of Johnson* and Southey's *Life of Nelson* to illustrate the point that historians, unlike Boswell and Southey, have stressed argument too much and narrative too little; they have not touched the feelings of readers nor stirred their imaginations. But these biographers have affected readers "without violating truth" and historians could do the same ("History," *Works*, VII, 211–12). The historian who aspires to be more than a polemicist should study another form, the novel. The example here is Sir Walter Scott, who has used "fragments of truth" ignored by historians, by which Macaulay means interesting details of ordinary life, such as those Scott chose to show how the

Puritans talked. A great historian would "reclaim those materials which the novelist has appropriated" (217). Macaulay uses the word "reclaim" here to indicate his belief that the classical historians were excellent narrators.

A more suggestive parallel for interpreting "Lord Clive," however, is Macaulay's comparison of historical writing to drama. After praising Tacitus for portraying real men rather than personifications of good and evil, he observes: "The talent which is required to write history thus bears a considerable affinity to the talent of a great dramatist. There is one obvious distinction. The dramatist creates: the historian only disposes. The difference is not in the mode of execution, but in the mode of conception" (197–98). It will be shown that the mode of execution in "Lord Clive" is dramatic.

Finally, an analogy to landscape painting is suggested by this statement: "History has its foreground and its background: and it is principally in the management of its perspective that one artist differs from another. Some events must be represented on a large scale, others diminished; the great majority will be lost in the dimness of the horizon; and a general idea of their joint effect will be given by a few slight touches" (178). Thucydides is praised for mastering this technique. A related principle is that selection and arrangement are as essential to historical writing as to other genres.

The same emphasis on narrative art appears in Macaulay's few but illuminating comments about his historical essays, as distinguished from statements on historical writing in general. The most important of these comments is the following, from a letter to Napier:

> The manner of these little historical essays bears, I think, the same analogy to the manner of Tacitus or Gibbon which . . . the manner of Shakespeare's historical plays [bears] to the manner of Sophocles. . . . The despair of Constance in Shakespeare is as lofty as that of Oedipus in Sophocles; but the levities of the bastard Faulconbridge would be utterly out of place in Sophocles. Yet we feel that they are not out of place in Shakespeare.
>
> So with these historical articles. Where the subject requires it, they may rise, if the author can manage it, to the highest altitudes of Thucydides. Then, again, they may without impropriety sink to the levity and colloquial ease of Horace Walpole's *Letters*. This is my theory. Whether I have succeeded in the execution is quite another question (18 April 1842; Trevelyan, II, 55–56).

Both the allusion to great dramatists in this passage and the defense of an informal tone are instructive.

Since Macaulay tended to picture men in action, he was drawn to the intrinsically dramatic events and figures of history. He chooses a single heroic character as the focus of an essay. Thus he writes to Napier while planning the Clive essay, "The subject is a grand one, and admits of decorations and illustrations innumerable" (4 July 1839; Pinney, III, 293). In another letter he rejects the idea of writing on Lord Cornwallis: "Clive and Hastings were great men, and their history is full of great events. Cornwallis was a respectable specimen of mediocrity" (14 July 1842; Trevelyan, II, 60-61). Great men and great events apparently required articles of greater scope than Macaulay's articles of the 1830s, which were usually from twenty to fifty pages. He requests seventy pages of the *Edinburgh Review* for Frederic the Great (18 April 1842; *Ibid*, p. 54).

Remarks in other letters indicate Macaulay's dramatic conception of the past. He calls historical figures in his articles "dramatis personae," for example, and complains, when planning an article on Edmund Burke that became instead a continuation of his study of Chatham, that "the stage is too small for the actors" (14 August 1844; *Ibid.*, p. 97). Similarly, in discussing his plan for the essay on Hastings, he lists the various "scenes" he imagines, adding that "the central figure is in the highest degree striking and majestic" (11 January 1841; Pinney, III, 61).

Concerned more with a great man's public life than with his private life, the historical essays are closer in spirit to dramas than to biographies, a distinction that becomes clear when one contrasts "Clive" or "Hastings" to the five *Encyclopaedia* articles Macaulay wrote in the 1850s. Actions described in the historical essays have the inevitable quality of actions unfolding in a play. The attention paid to Hastings' "striking and majestic" qualities affirms Macaulay's belief that the historical essay is primarily an artistic form, not a vehicle for instruction or political debate. Thus, although Hastings' case had been a cause célèbre, arousing support for the Indian governor as well as fierce opposition to him, Macaulay wrote neither a denunciation nor a eulogy, a fact that distinguishes the historical essays from such early argumentative works as "Milton."

The significance of Macaulay's defense of an informal tone, in the long passage quoted above, is that he wishes to establish the historical essay as a distinct genre. "This sort of composition has its own character, and its own laws," he tells Napier (18 April 1842; Trevelyan, II, 55). As a short story is not simply a little novel, the historical essay is not condensed history or abridged biography. That Macaulay saw the historical essay as both more interesting and more skillfully constructed than traditional histories or biographies is clear from allusions to Plutarch and Southey in letters to Napier. Macaulay professes to write "after the manner of Plutarch" in a letter dated 1 December 1841 (*Ibid.*, p. 54). And in the letter stating that the historical essay has its own character and can thus exhibit an informal tone that would be inappropriate for "regular" history, Macaulay says that Southey invented the historical essay, but that he has "in some points improved upon [Southey's] design" (18 April 1842; *Ibid.*, p. 55).

What did Macaulay mean by the statement that his historical essays were written "after the manner of Plutarch"? A letter written to T. F. Ellis from India gives a partial explanation: "I every now and then read one of Plutarch's *Lives* on an idle afternoon. . . . I like him prodigiously. . . . He tells a story delightfully, and his illustrations and sketches of character are as good as anything in ancient eloquence. I have never, till now, rated him fairly" (25 August 1835; Pinney, III, 153). The emphasis here is on narrative art. The reference to Plutarch is also clarified by Plutarch's introduction to the "Life of Alexander." In a famous passage, he states that his aim is not to give minute accounts of his subjects' lives, but rather "to epitomize the most celebrated parts of their story." Macaulay, too, prefers the epitome to the exhaustive account. Plutarch continues: "The most glorious exploits do not always furnish us with the clearest signs of virtue or vice in men; sometimes a matter of less moment, an expression or a jest, informs us better of their characters and inclinations than . . . the bloodiest battles."[7] Macaulay agrees that apparently trivial facts or actions can be very significant for the historian; and, like Plutarch, he uses anecdotes to illustrate character.

Despite these similarities between Plutarch and Macaulay, the historical essays differ in several respects from Plutarch's *Lives*. The edificatory purpose of the classical writer is much less discernible in Macaulay. A few early essays contain narrative passages in which Macaulay adopts a moralistic tone, but in such late works as "Hastings" and "Clive," his judgments are more tentative. The mean between extremes attitude that characterizes his politics, better demonstrated by "Gladstone" than by "Southey," extends by the time of the Clive essay to his moral judgments as well, so that

neither James Mill's harsh view of Clive nor the uncritical praise of
his biographer, Sir John Malcolm, strikes Macaulay as just. Since he
emphasizes heroic actions, his battle scenes are generally more detailed than Plutarch's. Another difference is that character revelation is more important to Plutarch than to Macaulay, who seldom
probes deeply into human conduct. Finally, his historical essays
differ from Plutarch's *Lives* in having a more formal and deliberately
rhetorical tone than the *Lives*, which preserve in translation
Plutarch's conversational tone. But when Macaulay notes that
Plutarch "tells a story delightfully," he states one of his own aims.

The modern parallel, to Southey, is not elaborated; but it is likely
that Macaulay had the *Life of Nelson* in mind when he said that
Southey invented the historical essay, because he had mentioned
the work in the essay "History" and had warmly praised it at the
beginning of "Southey's Colloquies" (*Works*, VII, 454). In any case,
Macaulay would have known that eighteenth century biographers
wrote long, extremely detailed works in which the subject was
eulogized, no matter how he had actually lived. Southey showed the
possibilities of a shorter form in the *Life of Nelson* (1813). First
published in the *Quarterly Review*, the work demonstrates skillful
selection and arrangement of materials. Southey announces his independence from the convention of eulogy by stating in the preface
that "the best eulogy of Nelson is the faithful history of his actions."
He adds, "the best history [is] that which shall relate them most
perspicuously."[8] The last word, meaning lucidly or intelligibly,
suggests Southey's concern for artistic narration, which is probably
the basis of Macaulay's statement that Southey invented the historical essay. A mere compiler or eulogist could not succeed in this
form.

How did Macaulay improve Southey's design? The comment may
be a general one, paraphrasing an earlier statement that Southey
was not as good "in designing as in filling up" the outline of a work
("Southey's Colloquies," *Works*, VII, 454). Or Macaulay may allude
to the dramatic quality of his essays, to the "bold, dashing, scene-
painting manner" which, he wrote to Napier, was best for periodical
works (20 July 1838; Pinney, III, 250). The art of transition
Macaulay considered one of the most important parts of historical
composition; he wrote in his journal that it was very hard "to make
the narrative flow along as it ought, every part naturally springing
from that which precedes" (15 April 1850; *Ibid.*, II, 211). By improv-

ing Southey's design, therefore, he may mean that his transitions are more skillful. In any event, Macaulay's method in "Lord Clive" illustrates his conception of the form that Southey invented.

### III  *"Lord Clive"*

The one hundred page essay on Robert Clive, founder of England's Indian Empire, is divided into three parts, corresponding to Clive's three trips to India, with sections on his returns to England concluding each part. Summarized in the last paragraphs, the events of the three trips comprise a drama in which the hero moves from adversity to prosperity to adversity. Like a dramatist, Macaulay includes details in the opening scenes that become more significant later. Recounting Clive's childhood, for example, he says that the boy's fearlessness seemed "hardly compatible with soundness of mind," (*Works*, IX, 189), a phrase that foreshadows suicide attempts and the severe depression that afflicted Clive late in life. In the first act, the obscure young Clive, bookkeeper turned soldier, triumphs at Arcot and returns to England a hero. The climax of the second act is his great victory at Plassey, which made him even more renowned. Since Clive is portrayed as a statesman as well as a general, his rise has a second peak, his successful attack on British corruption in Bengal. The third act, which describes Clive's Indian reforms and a parliamentary inquiry into his conduct, ends with his suicide. Moving gradually to this denouement, Macaulay slows the falling action at several points: (1) when, after Clive's spirited defense before the House of Commons, he receives only a mild censure; (2) when the treatment of Clive is favorably compared to the treatment of his rival, Joseph Dupleix, by the French; (3) when Macaulay suggests that, had Clive lived to fight in the American Revolution, the colonists might have been defeated; and (4) when Macaulay states that his genius sometimes "flashed through" the depression into which he sank during his last months. Careful not to exaggerate the contrast between Clive's brilliant career and unheroic death, Macaulay prepares for the end by noting that Clive had become addicted to opium and by describing his loss of energy through a simile: after his retirement, his "active spirit in an inactive situation drooped and withered like a plant in an uncongenial air" (282).

What follows the suicide may be considered an epilogue. Clive's achievements are summarized in the order of increasing importance: (1) English military power is established by the victories of his first trip to India; (2) England's political ascendancy dates from his second term; (3) honest administration begins with Clive's third trip. Thus, while the three parts of the essay bring Clive to his destruction, the three part epilogue establishes his claim to immortality. Macaulay's dramatic conception of the historical essay, evident in the structure of "Lord Clive," appears as well in his "scene-painting manner" and his characterization of Clive.

Macaulay's practice of scene painting follows his theoretical statement about foreground and background in historical composition: "some events must be represented on a large scale, others diminished" (VII, 178). The Black Hole of Calcutta scene is an example of the former. One hundred and forty-six English prisoners of Surajah Dowlah, the ruler of Bengal, are driven into a small prison cell called the Black Hole; only twenty-six survive. The passage begins with background details, Surajah Dowlah's hatred of the English and the flight of the English governor. Macaulay solemnly introduces the incident itself: "Then was committed that great crime, memorable for its singular atrocity, memorable for the tremendous retribution which followed" (IX, 222), and which led ultimately to English domination of India. In the following paragraphs, the sufferings of the prisoners are described, with interspersed references to Surajah Dowlah. The famous passage ends with terse sentences about a background figure which indirectly condemn the central figure, Surajah Dowlah: "One Englishwoman had survived that night. She was placed in the harem of the Prince at Moorshedabad" (224). Reference to an unnamed Englishwoman is one of the "slight touches" Macaulay recommends to give a general impression of events, in this case an impression of cruelty.

Inherently dramatic events are also chosen for other scenes: the siege of Arcot, the battle of Plassey, the conference following Surajah Dowlah's defeat, at which the scheming negotiator Omichund learns he has been duped by Clive, and the late scene in which Clive confronts English civil servants who hated him for his determination to root out abuses. Well-spaced throughout the essay, scenes keep attention focused on Clive, even when events not directly related to him but conveying a great fund of information about India are described. Throughout the essay, but especially in the battle scenes, Macaulay's diction conveys excitement. Clive's enemies at Arcot "rushed furiously to the attack," for example, and when fresh English troops reached the besieged Clive, he "instantly" took the offensive (209–10).

The dramatic technique of reversal, in which the opposite of what is expected occurs, is comparable to Macaulay's technique of listing many reasons why a particular event should not have happened as it did. And he makes Clive an improbable hero: his parents expected no good from their wild, untractable boy. Clive was "bred as a bookkeeper," Macaulay reminds us after describing his splendid victories, won over armies whose soldiers outnumbered his own twenty to one. Equally implausible were reforms he carried out in Bengal, where English corruption was widespread. Several times Macaulay contrasts the Indian Empire of his own day to India in the time of Clive, to suggest the improbable nature of the conquest, as well as to impress readers with England's achievement. This device is used far more extensively in the third chapter of the *History*, in which Victorian England is contrasted to England in 1685.

Exotic or bizarre details also contribute to the drama of "Lord Clive." Despondent during his first months in India, young Clive tries to shoot himself, but twice his loaded gun does not fire—details that foreshadow his suicide. The Moslem troops who storm the fort held by Clive at Arcot are drugged with bang, made from dried hemp leaves. At one point, Clive battles a pirate. At another, he walks through the treasury of Bengal, surrounded by gold and jewels and authorized to take whatever he wishes. These graphic details show Macaulay's eagerness to interest his readers in the conquest of India. Seven years before writing the Clive article, while preparing his great speech on the reorganization of Indian government, he was discouraged to find little public interest in Indian affairs.

Although not a "round" character, Clive is more fully delineated than characters in earlier narratives such as Burleigh, Hampden, and Temple. A fierce fighter, he is also humane, generous to friends, and magnanimous toward defeated rivals. Macaulay uses broad comparisons and contrasts to portray Clive. He begins by suggesting that Clive's story is as exciting as accounts of the great conquerors Hernando Cortez and Francisco Pizarro, a comparison that sets the tone of the essay. Clive is later likened to Julius Caesar, Napoleon, Trajan, Alexander the Great, General James Wolfe, and Sir William Bentinck; and Macaulay quotes Pitt, who said Clive was a military genius comparable to Frederic the Great. But Clive was also taken to epitomize the Nabobs, whose rapidly gained wealth from India and ostentatious display of it in England antagonized their countrymen. These parallels show that Macaulay's aim was not to reveal the main character's inner life but rather to create a dramatic context for his actions.

The chief foil to the protagonist is Dupleix, governor of French establishments in India, who plans operations but does not actually lead his troops in battle. Clive does both. A strong statement of his superiority to his rival comes, appropriately, at the end of the essay, when Macaulay says that by "dexterity and resolution" Clive accomplished more in India than Dupleix imagined possible. Less favorable to Clive is an implied contrast to one of his colleagues, Admiral Watson, who refuses to trick Omichund by signing a false treaty. Clive then forges his signature. On the other hand, Clive differs from the greedy English functionaries, whom Macaulay terms "ravenous adventurers." The hero declares in a letter, "I am come out with a mind superior to all corruption" and will end abuses or "perish in the attempt" (259). By quoting this letter to drive his point home rather than paraphrasing what he has previously said, Macaulay avoids the heavy emphasis of many passages in his early works.

There are other signs of a more varied prose style in "Lord Clive." Climax is used more naturally than in early works. When Macaulay writes, for example, that Clive "took Budgebudge, routed the garrison of Fort William . . . stormed and sacked Hoogley" (226), he slowly increases the emphasis

> took
> routed
> stormed and sacked,

without creating an exaggerated or strained effect. Similarly, words chosen to heighten the effect in battle scenes do not give a strident ring to the prose. In the sentence that introduces the action at Plassey, Macaulay creates a solemn impression through anaphora: "The day broke, the day which was to decide the fate of India" (233). Depicting the inhabitants of Bengal, he achieves a somber tone naturally: "The unhappy race never attempted resistance. Sometimes they submitted in patient misery. Sometimes they fled from the white man, as their fathers had been used to fly from the

Mahratta; and the palanquin of the English traveller was often carried through silent villages and towns, which the report of his approach had made desolate" (256).

This passage not only shows Macaulay's humanitarian spirit and puts Clive's military deeds into a larger context, it also illustrates the idea that the historical essay's tone may rise to solemnity or fall to a colloquial level, whichever is appropriate. An example of the latter comes when Clive complains that Parliament has treated him like a sheepstealer (277). Macaulay expresses his enemies' hope that he would lose his knighthood by saying that these men wished "to see his spurs chopped off" (276). Metaphors are more suggestive in the Clive essay than in earlier works. When public opinion turns against the Nabobs and the India company, Macaulay says, "The whole storm, which had long been gathering, now broke at once on the head of Clive" (275). Like other transitional statements in the work, this one shows Macaulay's use of "prospective and retrospective summaries."[9] These summaries unify the narrative while creating a sense of movement.

Another sign of a more artistic prose style than is found in earlier works, besides the passages that point both forward and backward, is the symbolic meaning that Macaulay gives to a column erected by Dupleix to mark one of his victories. Later Clive orders his men to destroy the pompously inscribed column, an act that signals the appearance of a new military power, England, and reveals as well that Clive is destined to be an even more striking and dominant figure than Dupleix. The column symbol reinforces two important contrasts in the essay: real power versus nominal power and imperialistic ruthlessness (represented by both the French and the English) versus the enlightened policies of Clive.

Finally, ironic touches in the essay add to its fullness and complexity. Clive succeeded in purifying Indian government, but old abuses were revived after he left, a commentary on human ambition (272). Then he runs afoul of British public opinion and Parliament, not because of his few misdeeds but because of his "determined resistance to avarice and tyranny" (278). Ironically, the virtues of the reformer turn out to be political liabilities. And he was held responsible for abuses that he had in fact opposed.

Clive's military career lent itself to dramatic presentation, but Macaulay faced the difficulty of recounting his later life in such a way that it would be interesting and would seem related to his conquests. One effective resolution of the problem is emphasizing the many obstacles Clive had to overcome in fighting corruption and defending himself in England. Macaulay also uses military imagery effectively to make Clive's later life seem heroic. We read for example that although his reforms met with strong opposition, "all resistance was quelled" (260). Turning to the investigation of Indian affairs in the House of Commons, Macaulay writes, "Clive's parliamentary tactics resembled his military tactics. Deserted, surrounded, outnumbered, and with everything at stake, he did not even deign to stand on the defensive, but boldly pushed forward to the attack" (276). This picture stresses Clive's courage and recalls earlier scenes.

Like most works of Macaulay, "Lord Clive" has been praised but not analyzed.[10] Seeing it in the light of Macaulay's idea of the historical essay helps us to understand why it is an effective work. "Lord Clive" and the other historical essays, "Hastings," "Frederic the Great," and "The Earl of Chatham," show that Macaulay's talent was better suited to narration than to argument, although we have seen that "Civil Disabilities of the Jews" and "Gladstone" are persuasive and skillfully constructed works. What Macaulay says about the *Life of Nelson* fits the Clive essay as well: "The character of the hero lay on the surface. The exploits were brilliant and picturesque" ("Southey's Colloquies," *Works*, VII, 454). To transform this material into a unified narrative, Macaulay exploited its dramatic possibilities and thereby gave the historical essay a strengthened claim to be considered as a distinctive genre. He believed that the impact of a single man upon history was limited; yet he loved to imagine the great scenes of the past, and the central figures of his historical essays are heroes who illustrate, to some degree, the Carlylean definition of history as the biographies of great men. At the same time that we recognize the epic dimension of the central characters in "Lord Clive" and "Warren Hastings," however, we are made to feel that powerful and impersonal forces clash in the struggle for Indian supremacy. The drama of that struggle is Macaulay's theme in "Lord Clive."

### CHAPTER 6

# *"Addison" and "Madame D'Arblay"*

MACAULAY would have found the highly specialized literary scholarship of the present constricting, for he liked to expatiate upon a writer's life and times and digress to related topics. His "critical" essays are not primarily critical, but argumentative or biographical. Such general studies were usual for the Victorian periodical writer, who reached a wide audience, but were particularly well-suited to Macaulay, because he had a poor opinion of his critical ability. With characteristic exaggeration he told Napier: "I have never written a page of criticism on poetry, or the fine arts, which I would not burn if I had the power" (26 June 1838; Pinney, III, 245). Although Macaulay's criticism lacks the brilliance of his best narrative and polemical works, it is often stimulating and perceptive. But the criticism has usually been represented by the pronouncements of his earliest essays. Thus two of his last and best *Edinburgh* essays, those on Fanny Burney and Joseph Addison, deserve special notice.

## I  *Early Criticism*

Like Samuel Johnson, Macaulay assumes a judicial attitude toward writers, telling why their work deserves praise or blame. His tone is formal because he considers the discrimination of beauties and faults an important public duty in an age when the middle class reading audience was greatly increasing. Thus in his article on the poetaster Robert Montgomery, he attacks the practice of "puffing" books and assures *Edinburgh* readers that an author needs more than a pious subject to be successful. He also urges readers to value clarity; one of his critical principles is that affectation and obscurity are the worst faults of style. That is why he upbraids Montgomery for the imprecision of these lines from *The Omnipresence of the Deity:*

79

Oh! Never did the dark-soul'd Atheist stand,
And watch the breakers boiling on the strand,
And, while Creation stagger'd at his nod,
Mock the dread presence of the mighty God!

The lines bring out Macaulay's sense of the ludicrous, since Creation apparently staggers at the nod of the atheist. Like an eighteenth century satirist, Macaulay attacks Montgomery for pretentious and clumsy moralizing. He finds no satanic qualities in the protagonist of Montgomery's *Satan,* and advises the author to change a few lines and republish the poem with the title *Gabriel.*

Since eighteenth century tastes and values are reflected throughout Macaulay's work, it is not surprising that two seemingly contradictory ideas that were often intertwined in the eighteenth century, primitivism and progress,[1] appear in critical passages of the early essays. Macaulay believes that literary criticism is a progressive science. More important, he argues in "Milton" and "Dryden" that poetry declines as civilization progresses: "In proportion as men know more and think more, they look less at individuals and more at classes. They therefore make better theories and worse poems" ("Milton," *Works,* VII, 7). The sharp antithesis of theories to poems assumes a conflict between reason and imagination and equates civilization with reason alone. Macaulay falls into this oversimplification because his understanding of poetic illusion is very narrow. The power of illusion creates impressions that are literally false, in his view; they are not merely the poet's interpretations of reality. Poets therefore resemble children. To argue that imaginative power is strongest in children, Macaulay states that the emotional impact of Little Red Riding Hood upon a child is greater than the impact of Lear or Hamlet upon an adult (8). His notion of poetry as illusion and illusion as error is also conveyed through this analogy: "Poetry produces an illusion on the eye of the mind, as a magic lantern produces an illusion on the eye of the body. And, as the magic lantern acts best in a dark room, poetry effects its purpose most completely in a dark age. . . . We cannot unite the incompatible advantages of reality and deception . . ." (9). Here the contrast between reality and deception restates the theories versus poems contrast noted above. The simple physical process represented by the magic lantern obscures rather than explains poetic effect.

The source of the idea that poetry declines with the advance of civilization, an idea that virtually disappears from Macaulay's writing after 1828, has been traced to various individual writers—William Hazlitt, Thomas Peacock, Francis Jeffrey—and more generally to the intellectual milieu of the eighteenth century.[2] A Utilitarian influence can also be suggested. When Macaulay refers in the same sentence to Little Red Riding Hood and King Lear, he fails to distinguish between the kinds of pleasure offered by the two works. Utilitarians were often censured for overlooking differences among pleasures. Bentham's comparison of pushpin to poetry is well known. Without adopting the Utilitarians' condescending view of poetry, Macaulay reflects their attitudes by sharply opposing reason and imagination and by declaring in the Milton essay that the poetic imagination reaches its greatest perfection "in a rude state of society" (8). Bentham had described poetry as the "production of a rude age."[3]

Macaulay returns to this theme in "Dryden" (1828), where it receives much-needed qualification. Here he says that poetic excellence results not merely from imaginative vigor but from the skillful use of language (VII, 127). The golden age of poetry comes therefore not in its first age, as claimed in "Milton," but at a somewhat later time when language has become more highly developed (129). Further, Macaulay now suggests that reason and imagination are not necessarily antithetical; besides a strong imagination, the poet needs information and experience to communicate effectively (127). The early, creative age of poetry is distinguished from a subsequent critical age, to which Dryden belongs. Since the later age is inferior, by Macaulay's definition, Dryden cannot be ranked among the greatest poets, although his satires are praised.

More important than the kinds of literary judgments Macaulay offers in the Milton and Dryden essays is the fact that the works are primarily arguments in which critical passages are subordinate. Thus it is difficult to be certain that he would not have written differently in purely expository works. Apparently he abandoned the theory that poetry declines as civilization develops when he no longer needed it to prove a point. The purpose of this argument in "Milton" is to magnify Milton's achievement. "No poet has ever triumphed over greater difficulties" because the age of creative power poetry was long past when Milton wrote (VII, 10). To praise

the Whigs and attack the Tories, Macaulay seeks to characterize
Milton as favorably as possible.[4] Treating Milton's conduct sympathetically is meant to suggest to readers that public men can
attack the status quo and still be patriotic, a Whig message Macaulay
is eager to impart at a time when advocates of Reform were considered dangerous.

Since Macaulay's primary concern in his early essays is to win
debates and not to elaborate critical theories, some inconsistencies
naturally appear in his statements. In "Byron" he ranks Romantic
poetry above Augustan, an apparent contradiction of the idea that
poetry declines as civilization progresses. In an article on Dante
written for *Knight's Quarterly* in 1824 he states, "The finest works of
imagination have always been produced in times of political convulsion" (XI, 261). But political convulsion occurs in all ages, not
merely in the primitive stage when, according to "Milton," poetry
reaches its highest development. In "Dante," Macaulay contrasted
the precise details used by the Italian poet to describe supernatural
characters with Milton's "vague sublimity," judging Dante's method
to be the more effective. But when he makes the same contrast in
"Milton" one year later, he says that he will not choose between the
two poets (VII, 20); since he has introduced the parallel to focus
attention on Milton's greatness, he would weaken his argument by
placing Dante above Milton. If Macaulay had a coherent theory of
poetry, such shifts would not occur.

Although he argues many points in "Byron"—for example, that
Byron links Romantic poetry to Augustan—the criticism in this
essay is not primarily a vehicle for debate. "Byron" gives a broader
view of Macaulay's literary opinions than either "Milton" or "Dryden." The influence of Romanticism is clear, for example. Macaulay
uses the eighteenth century terms "correctness" and "just imitation
of nature," paradoxically, to defend Wordsworth, Percy Bysshe
Shelley, Samuel Taylor Coleridge, and Byron; the terms apparently
mean creative power. Disparaging the traditional view of correctness, Macaulay shows an impatience with rules of composition that
is clearly romantic. And an eloquent passage describing the power
and range of poetry (VII, 549–50) seems to come from his own
experience of poetry, whereas the less effective criticism of "Milton"
and "Dryden" is abstract. Macaulay understands the importance of
organic unity, a principle stressed by Coleridge. He notes in the
Byron essay for example that remarkable as Hamlet's soliloquies are

when excerpted from the play, they are even more remarkable as parts of the whole (563). Similarly, he attacks abridged and expurgated editions of great books in the first Samuel Johnson essay (VIII, 76).

Macaulay differs from the Romantics in two important respects, however. Passages in the essays on Milton and Dryden in which he refers to "imagination" indicate that he uses the term in the older sense of image-making power and does not mean by it a creative, unifying faculty. Secondly, he dislikes personal revelations. Thus he praises Milton and Dante for concealing "the nakedness and sores of their minds," unlike egotistical modern poets ("Milton," VII, 27). But he writes sympathetically of Byron's suffering; the poet's gloomy descriptions of himself do not interfere with Macaulay's appreciation of his poetry, which was first expressed many years earlier in letters to his parents (Pinney, I, 47; 65–66).

A strength of the essay is Macaulay's ability to consider Byron's poetry on its own merit, without letting the facts of Byron's personal life color his judgment. Macaulay is a didactic critic in that he seeks to instruct. But in contrast to Jeffrey, who wrote harshly of Byron, Macaulay merely notes in passing that some young readers took from Byron's work an ethical system "in which the two great commandments were, to hate your neighbour and to love your neighbour's wife" (569). But the fault lies as much with the readers as with the writer. Bryon's characters are variations of himself Macaulay observes, and his dialogue tends to become soliloquy (561–62). But his descriptive power and his ability to communicate intense feeling are noted as well. Byron's work can be judged fairly only in later times, when it can be separated from his life, Macaulay declares, but he astutely predicts that Byron will be seen as one of England's greatest poets.

In "Milton" and "Dryden," and to a lesser extent in "Byron," Macaulay tends to discuss literature in relation to other subjects rather than to describe the particular qualities of works or the development of a writer's style. Instead of concentrating upon Milton, for example, he considers Milton's resemblance to Dante; and Byron's role as a transitional poet interests him as much as the distinguishing features of his individual works. Biographical criticism as opposed to formal criticism operates in such ways, of course, but it is characteristic of Macaulay to work around a topic rather than to penetrate beneath its surface. For this reason, much of his criticism

seems rather thin. "Horace Walpole" (1833) is divided into a critical
section and a historical section on Robert Walpole, and the essay
becomes noticeably more lively when Macaulay turns from literature to politics. But ten years later, after developing his narrative art
to a high degree, Macaulay returned to criticism. The essays
"Madame D'Arblay" (Fanny Burney) and "Addison" suggest that
this development aided his criticism, for in them he focuses more
directly than before on the subject at hand and is therefore more
detailed and informative in his commentary.

## II  Madame D'Arblay (1843)

*Memoirs of Doctor Burney,* a work about her father that Fanny
Burney published when she was eighty, was attacked in the *Quarterly Review* for April 1833 by Macaulay's enemy John Wilson
Croker, who ridiculed her prose style and accused her of lying about
her age when she published *Evelina.* These accusations became
especially troubling to Fanny Burney in the months before her
death in 1840, and her niece wrote to Macaulay asking if he would
answer Croker. Stating his admiration for Burney, he politely refused to be her champion: "Her place in public estimation will be
fixed," he assured her niece, "not by what other people may write
about her but by what she has written herself." Burney thanked
Macaulay, saying that she would have "gladly accepted [her] vindi-
cation from his hand."[5] Two years later, the appearance of the *Diary
and Letters of Madame D'Arblay* gave Macaulay a chance to vindicate her after all, not by attacking Croker directly, in the abusive
manner of his 1831 review of Croker's edition of Boswell, but by
concentrating on the novelist's merit. Macaulay felt genuine affec-
tion for Fanny Burney, but probably treated her with special favor
because a few months before his article appeared, she had been
attacked a second time by Croker.[6]

The first part of Macaulay's essay describes Fanny Burney's early
life, and the second evaluates her works; but the parts are not
sharply opposed, for characteristics of the novels are mentioned in
the biographical section of the review. We get a fuller impression of
Burney, both as a person and a novelist, than of writers Macaulay
treated earlier because scenes as well as summaries portray her. We
see her shyly observing people from different social classes at Dr.
Burney's musical parties; talking to his friend Samuel Johnson; destroying her first stories at the command of her stepmother; waiting

on Queen Charlotte, wife of George III; watching the trial of Warren Hastings; and meeting Mme de Staël, Tallyrand, and others
exiled by the French Revolution. Macaulay delights in the improbability of her success: an obscure young woman anonymously pub-
lishes *Evelina*, the best novel to appear since Smollett's death
(*Works*, X, 21). A darker side of Fanny Burney's life, her five year
service to the queen, arouses Macaulay's indignation because she
was unable to complete any novels during this time and because the
idea of her servitude angers him.

Macaulay takes Fanny Burney seriously as an artist, a point to be
stressed since women writers were treated condescendingly in the
nineteenth century, with such tags as "lady novelist" persisting in
the twentieth century as well. The attention paid to Burney's art
suggests that Macaulay, an enthusiastic novel reader, regards the
end of fiction as pleasure rather than moral uplift. Writing anonymously in the *Christian Observer* when he was sixteen, Macaulay
stressed the edifying possibilities of the novel, but may have taken
this tack solely to reassure the Evangelical readers and his father,
Zachary, the editor.[7] Three years later in a letter to Zachary, he
defends literature that merely entertains, in response to Zachary's
criticism that his Cambridge prize poem "Pompeii" lacked a moral
(5 February 1819; Pinney, I, 119).

According to Macaulay, Burney's first two novels, *Evelina* and
*Cecilia*, are superior to her later works. Some of the best qualities of
the novels are also to be found in her diary and letters: observation
of detail, skillful grouping of characters, and a lively comic spirit
(*Works*, X, 21). Macaulay also praises her inventiveness, the suit-
ability of her plots to her characters, and the clear, natural style in
which she wrote her first novels. Later she began to imitate Samuel
Johnson, with disastrous results: "In an evil hour the author of
*Evelina* took *The Rambler* for her model" (62). Macaulay does not
object to Johnson's style per se, only to its use for fiction. He then
distinguishes three styles in Fanny Burney, quoting passages to
illustrate and thereby providing more specific criticism than is found
in "Milton" or "Dryden." *Evelina* and *Cecilia* represent the early,
natural style of Fanny Burney. She then wrote *Camilla* (1796) in
Johnson's manner. Finally, after her marriage to D'Arblay, she lived
in France for many years; and, as a result of speaking and thinking in
French, she wrote "a sort of broken Johnsonese" (64). Macaulay may
exaggerate the corrupting influence of Johnson upon Burney, but he

draws the inference from the works themselves, rather than append-
ing the works to broad generalizations as he does in the essays on
Milton and Dryden.

Another difference in the Fanny Burney essay is that the parallels
Macaulay chooses for amplification seem more closely related to the
main subject and less elaborate than their counterparts in early
works. This is seen in the most interesting critical passage of the
1843 essay, a discussion of characterization, the aim of which is to
define Fanny Burney's art. Like Ben Jonson, she excels in drawing
humour characters, men and women who display one dominant
trait. Although creating them does not require the highest art, "a
writer may show so much genius in the exhibition of these humours
as to be fairly entitled to a distinguished and permanent rank among
classics" (59). Such is the case with Fanny Burney, whom Macaulay
praises for the great variety of the humors found among her characters.

Without setting up a sharp contrast, he describes the more excellent kind of character delineation, using a striking parallel between
Shakespeare and Jane Austen to illustrate his meaning. Shakespeare's variety, he says,

is like the variety of nature, endless diversity, scarcely any monstrosi-
ty. . . . The silly notion that every man has one ruling passion . . . finds no
countenance in the plays of Shakespeare. There man appears as he is, made
up of a crowd of passions, which contend for the mastery over him, and
govern him in turn. . . . Admirable as he was in all parts of his art, we most
admire him for this, that while he has left us a greater number of striking
portraits than all other dramatists put together, he has scarcely left us a
single caricature. (57–58)

To a lesser degree the same is true of Jane Austen, who was not as
highly regarded in the nineteenth century as she is today. Macaulay
names four of her clergymen, noting how similar they are in out-
ward circumstances but how easily distinguishable from one
another. Thus the great subtlety of Austen's character drawing is
emphasized. Henry James may have had this passage in mind when
he described Macaulay as Austen's "first slightly ponderous
amoroso."[8] Or he may have recalled a statement in Trevelyan: Austen's novels "remained without a rival in [Macaulay's] affec-
tions. . . . In 1858 he notes in his journal, 'If I could get materials, I
really would write a short life of that wonderful woman and raise a

little money to put up a monument to her in Winchester Cathedral' " (Trevelyan, II, 389).

A short life of Austen by Macaulay would probably have been even warmer than his literary biography of Fanny Burney. When he says that we owe *Mansfield Park* as well as *Evelina* to her, he indicates her influence on Austen. Macaulay gives other reasons for Burney's importance in the history of English fiction. Novels had been considered immoral, a stigma that did not wholly disappear in the nineteenth century, but she demonstrated that high-spirited comedy involving even low characters could be thoroughly wholesome. Moreover, *Evelina* was the first novel by a woman that deserved to live; its author therefore "vindicated the right of her sex to an equal share in a fair and noble province of letters" (*Works*, X, 71). By celebrating not only Fanny Burney but the novel itself, Macaulay performs in his essay the task Matthew Arnold later set for the critic, to "propagate the best that is known and thought in the world."[9] In 1903, when Fanny Burney was ushered into a rather exclusive male club, the English Men of Letters series, Macaulay received most of the credit for establishing her literary reputation.[10]

## III   *Addison (1843)*

Unlike Samuel Johnson's "Addison" in *Lives of the English Poets* and Macaulay's essay on Fanny Burney, which are divided into sections of biography and criticism, Macaulay's "Life and Writings of Addison" includes no separate section of criticism. Although many of Addison's works are described, the essay is primarily biographical, not critical. It is far more detailed than Johnson's account but resembles it in demonstrating the author's later, less elaborately rhetorical style. In the same year that he wrote "Addison," Macaulay admitted in the preface to his collected *Edinburgh* works that he found "Milton," written eighteen years earlier in 1825, "overloaded with gaudy and ungraceful ornament" (*Works*, VII, xii). The same cannot be said of "Addison." The style of "Addison," though plainer than that of "Milton," is still formal and stately, however, as Virginia Woolf makes clear at the beginning of her essay on Addison when she writes that Macaulay's assertions remind her "of a Prime Minister making a proclamation on behalf of a great empire." Woolf's short essay is written in a far different spirit—conversational, personal, whimsical. Both Johnson and Macaulay had reported with approval that Addison, on his deathbed, summoned his wife's rakish young son, Lord Warwick, so that he could see how a Christian dies. Alluding to this scene, Woolf says that the sympathies of the modern reader are more likely to be with Warwick than with Addison, who was "not too far gone for a last spasm of self complacency."[11]

Comparing Macaulay's essay to a monument and praising it as one of his most vigorous works, Woolf suggests that the reader is likely to wonder, nevertheless, if it is true. She quotes a few exaggerated statements from the essay, saying that out of context they appear "grotesque." But in context, "such is the persuasive power of design—they are part of the decoration; they complete the monument."[12] Woolf gives a good introduction to Macaulay's "Addison" by calling attention to this problem, which was recently posed in another way: is it possible to tell the truth in Macaulay's style?[13] There is certainly a falsifying element in his rhetoric, but a reader conscious of it can enjoy the "decoration" without being misled by it. One may also substitute truths for truth, acknowledging that the truths of human behavior that the best novelists disclose cannot be found in Macaulay and that the careful distinctions of such prose writers as John Henry Newman and John Ruskin are beyond him, while at the same time pointing out that he conveys truths about public life, about the interplay of characters and events.

Thus "Addison" is a masterful narrative of a career in the first years of the eighteenth century. Since actions reveal character, Macaulay is able to draw a broad sketch of Addison the private man, but it is only a sketch. Like Macaulay, Addison was famous both as a Whig politician and as a man of letters. Very few major English writers have held cabinet posts; Addison and Macaulay have that in common. After his marriage, Addison lived at Holland House, where Macaulay was later to be distinguished in Whig society by his talk and his learning. No doubt aware of these parallels, Macaulay writes warmly of Addison, whose politics and moderation he greatly admires. He shows his own moderation by treating the book that occasioned his review, Lucy Aiken's *Life and Writings of Addison,* far more gently in the pages of the *Edinburgh Review* than in his letters to Napier.

Macaulay condenses a great deal of information about Addison and his times into a relatively short space. We learn of the influence of the press on public opinion, England's foreign relations, Whig and Tory domestic politics, the place of oratory in seventeenth century politics as contrasted to nineteenth century politics, the state of newspapers, and the history of Magdalene College. Surrounding the main character are many statesmen and writers whose place in his life is described: George Halifax, John Somers, Thomas Wharton, Sidney Godolphin, Richard Steele, Jonathan Swift, Alexander Pope, John Dryden, and Nicolas Boileau. Macaulay works in disagreements with Johnson and Aiken on a few points: the sincerity of Boileau's praise of Addison's Latin poems; the strength of his classical background; and his treatment of Steele. The success of the essay depends partly on this fullness and partly on the ease with which transitions are made. From Addison's youthful praise of Dryden, for example, Macaulay moves to Dryden's introduction of Addison to William Congreve, who presented him to Charles Montagu, later Lord Halifax, a Whig leader. Having introduced these narrative threads, the influence of powerful men on Addison's career and his choice of the Whig party, Macaulay does not develop them until later in the essay. Thus a kind of foreshadowing can be seen in "Addison," as in "Lord Clive." The reader scarcely notices that the narrative moves back and forth between the details of Addison's career and the politics and social history of his age.

But the vigor of "Addison" comes not only from its condensed effect and its narrative flow, but also from its concreteness. As if to illustrate his remark that the particular has an advantage over the general ("Addison," *Works*, X, 107), Macaulay says that as a writer on common life and manners, Addison preceded the great novelists of the century: when Addison wrote for the *Spectator* "Richardson was working as a compositor. Fielding was robbing birds' nests. Smollett was not yet born" (133). And to describe Addison's attempt to reform Warwick he writes, "The great wit and scholar tried to allure the young Lord from the fashionable amusements of beating watchmen, breaking windows, and rolling women in hogsheads [casks] down Holborn Hill . . ." (157).

Macaulay's prose is concrete in the early essays, too, and although "Addison" is less florid and more tightly constructed than "Milton" or "Southey," and superior to the first part of "Bacon" as a biographical study, it has qualities besides concreteness in common with works of the 1820s and 1830s. In "Addison," for example, we see the familiar rhetorical device of heightening the praise bestowed on one person by disparaging others. It seems that Macaulay could be fair to only one person at a time. Addison is portrayed as admira-

ble, while Swift, Pope, and Steele are introduced mainly to embody
disagreeable traits, thereby to serve as foils to Addison. An incident
concerning Steele shows Macaulay's bias. He recalls that Addison
once sent a bailiff to collect money he had loaned to Steele, an act
that to some showed Addison abusing his friend and collaborator. To
defend Addison with no evidence but his imagination, Macaulay
pictures Steele squandering the borrowed money on a lavish feast.

Besides a rather superficial use of foils, the essay reveals a weakness seen in the magic lantern analogy which explains poetic effect,
the use of a simple physical parallel for a complex idea or process. To
stress the notion that it was easier to write fluent heroic couplets
after Pope, Macaulay says that later eighteenth century writers
could easily "manufacture" heroic couplets, making them as smooth
and as alike as blocks that have passed through a mill (X, 83). But
since this is the only example in "Addison" of the simplifying
method commonly found in early works, it indicates an improvement in Macaulay's prose style.

In addition, the literary criticism of "Addison," like that of
"Madame D'Arblay," is more informative than that of "Milton" or
"Dryden" and is free from the cleverly elaborated but superficial
theories of poetry expounded in those early articles. Works are
taken up chronologically and related to Addison's life. As before,
Macaulay sees the critic's task as one of ranking, i.e., distinguishing
the best works from lesser works within an author's canon and in
comparison to other writers' works; *Cato*, for example, is inferior to
Greek drama, Elizabethan drama, and the best of Schiller, but is
superior to some of Pierre Corneille and Jean Racine. But Macaulay
now pays more attention to the characteristics of individual works.
And when he introduces a parallel to Swift and Voltaire to define the
special quality of Addison's humor, its delicacy and humanity, the
parallel is drawn rather briefly. Held up as the best English essayist,
Addison is praised for awakening in readers a sense of the ludicrous
through ordinary events and characters. A careful observer, he
could communicate what he saw either by describing traits or by
inventing characters. The *Spectator* can be reread many times. Its
essays are good individually but can also be seen as parts of a whole.

Macaulay's command of literary history is evident from several of
his explanations. The simile of the angel guiding the whirlwind in
"The Campaign" gained part of its effect, he notes for example, from
a storm that caused great destruction in England in November of

1703. In Venice, Addison saw a play on the death of Cato that inspired his famous drama of the same name. When Cato was first performed, Macaulay tells us, Steele took the precaution of packing the house. A passage in one of Addison's Latin poems is suggested as the source of a passage in *Gulliver's Travels*. We learn how the *Tatler* and the *Spectator* were begun. From the circulation of the *Spectator*, Macaulay estimates that Addison was as widely read in his time as Scott and Dickens in the nineteenth century.

Macaulay found Addison a more congenial subject than Byron, Southey, or Horace Walpole, and the praise of Addison specialists for his essay indicates its success.[14] Aside from its interest as a lively narrative, Macaulay's "Addison," like the essays of Samuel Johnson and Virginia Woolf, presents the opinion of one major English writer about another. As Woolf observes, Macaulay's essay is a monument to Addison, but it is also a Victorian document to the extent that it celebrates Addison's moral earnestness. Macaulay was occasionally attacked for paying insufficient attention to morality, and it is true that his works, taken as a whole, do not reflect the religious world view of Clapham with which he grew up. But his writings evince a broadly Christian morality, which is somewhat more obvious in "Addison" than in many of his other *Edinburgh Review* articles. He speaks of the "moral purity" of Addison's satire, for example, and notes approvingly that Addison did not mock religion. At a time of fierce political warfare, he "blackened no man's character" (126). Moreover, his essays had a moral use: they undermined an idea left over from the Restoration that immorality and cleverness go hand in hand. "So effectually, indeed, did he retort on vice the mockery which had recently been directed against virtue, that, since his time, the open violation of decency has always been considered among us as a mark of a fool" (127). Macaulay adds that this was the greatest revolution ever accomplished by a satirist, and declares in the last sentence of the review that Addison "reconciled wit and virtue" (167). The literary value of Addison's works for Macaulay, then, depends at least partly on the purifying role they played in the early eighteenth century.

Other Victorians wrote more penetrating criticism than Macaulay; nothing of his can compare to Ruskin's analysis of "Lycidas" in *Sesame and Lilies* or Arnold's "The Function of Criticism at the Present Time." But no writer has communicated a love for literature with greater energy. That is the chief merit of Macaulay's criticism, and it is more evident in the essays on Fanny Burney and Addison than in such early works as "Milton" and "Dryden." His criticism changes its emphasis rather than develops: when it is part of a narrative work, as in the late essays, it is more substantial than when it appears in the context of argument. Just as Macaulay preferred the "exact details of Dante [to] the dim intimations of Milton" (*Works*, VII, 19), his readers are likely to prefer his detailed accounts of eighteenth century writers to the more abstract commentary of the early, argumentative essays.

CHAPTER 7

# "Samuel Johnson"

I Encyclopaedia Britannica *Articles 1853–1859*

THE decade of the 1850s was a time of special prosperity for Macaulay, as it was for England. The wealth, progress, and optimism of the Victorian age, especially of the 1850s, were symbolized by the Great Exhibition of 1851, while the symbol of Macaulay's personal achievement was a peerage. When he became Baron Macaulay of Rothley in 1857, choosing the title from his birthplace, he moved to the House of Lords from the House of Commons, to which Edinburgh voters had sent him in 1852. They had shown their high regard for Macaulay by electing him even though he had not been a candidate. In 1855, publication of volumes three and four of the *History of England* increased his fame. He died at the end of 1859 and was buried in Westminster Abbey.

By marshaling evidence for the "development hypothesis," as the Victorians called evolution, a work published in the same year that Macaulay died, Darwin's *Origin of Species*, makes a sharp break with the past. By contrast, the five works Macaulay wrote between the years 1853 and 1859 recall the static world of the eighteenth century. The subjects of these biographical essays, written for the *Encyclopaedia Britannica* at the request of Macaulay's friend Adam Black, are John Bunyan and four eighteenth century figures: Francis Atterbury, Oliver Goldsmith, William Pitt, and Samuel Johnson. The prose style of the shorter works, "Atterbury," "Bunyan," and "Goldsmith," is plainer than that of Macaulay's *Edinburgh Review* essays, and can be compared to Johnson's style in *Lives of the Poets*. The longer articles, "William Pitt" and "Samuel Johnson," on the other hand, more closely resemble Macaulay's periodical works, especially "Addison."

The subject of the first *Encyclopaedia* article is Francis Atterbury, Tory bishop and polemicist who was imprisoned and later banished for his part in Jacobite conspiracies. Macaulay is unable to treat Atterbury's political life with complete fairness, but his Whig bias is less pronounced in 1853 than it had been in the 1820s. In his next article he writes more sympathetically of Bunyan's religious zeal than he had of Atterbury's intrigues. A sign that Macaulay's arguments can be distinguished from narrative essays is that two generalizations made in an 1831 *Edinburgh* article on Bunyan are not repeated in the biographical sketch of 1854: *Pilgrim's Progress* is the only allegory that has a strong human interest, and "Bunyan is almost the only writer who ever gave to the abstract the interest of the concrete" (*Works*, VII, 607; 610). The third article, "Goldsmith" (1856), shows Macaulay's limited insight into men different from himself, a shortcoming he may have recognized when he wrote at the end of the essay: "A life of Goldsmith would have been an inestimable addition to the *Lives of the Poets*. No man appreciated Goldsmith's writings more justly than Johnson: no man was better acquainted with Goldsmith's character and habits; and no man was more competent to delineate with truth and spirit the peculiarities of a mind in which great powers were found in company with great weaknesses" (X, 442). This tribute is somewhat weakened by Macaulay's suggestion that Johnson, too, had great failings.

The limits of the antithetical manner for character drawing are quite evident here: men as different from one another as Goldsmith and Johnson are reduced to a single similarity. Yet Goldsmith is a more sympathetic character in this essay than he had been in 1831, when Macaulay dismissed him as an "inspired idiot" ("Samuel Johnson," VIII, 80). In one of his Indian minutes, Macaulay described Goldsmith's histories of Greece and Rome as "miserable performances" (Trevelyan, I, 378), but his opinion has changed by 1856: he now praises Goldsmith for the "clear, pure, and flowing language" of the histories and for mastery of the narrative arts of selection and condensation (*Works*, X, 436–37).

In the Whig statesman William Pitt, Macaulay finds a subject with whom he can more readily identify. He had earlier devoted two *Edinburgh* articles to the elder Pitt, Earl of Chatham. The 1859 biography of the younger Pitt is Macaulay's last work. Much longer than the lives of Atterbury, Bunyan, and Goldsmith, "William Pitt" has three main divisions, two narrative sections separated by a section of analysis. The first part (X, 489–516) ends in 1784, with the twenty-five year old Pitt at the height of his fame; Macaulay then discusses the strengths and weaknesses of parliamentary government as Pitt's career reflects them, the characteristics of Pitt's oratory, his domestic life, the reasons for his popularity, and his failure to patronize the arts (516–28); the last section (528–64) takes the chronological account of Pitt's career from 1784 to his death in 1806.

Macaulay's vast knowledge of eighteenth century politics gives this work a complexity not found in earlier essays. Although he imposes a pattern upon the material, choosing to emphasize Pitt's success in the first section and his defeats and failures in the third, the pattern is flexible enough to allow for variation. The great victory of Trafalgar comes in the midst of Pitt's reverses in part three, for example. Neither a hero nor a villain, Pitt is presented as a defender of civil and religious liberty and a champion of reform, who is compelled by circumstances to head a repressive government in the years following the French Revolution. Pitt is a more believable character than Macaulay's Addison. The summary of his career is a model of concise prose (563–64). Macaulay's language usually does not convey a sense of mystery or profound sadness, but a notable exception is the description of Pitt's funeral.

## II   *Samuel Johnson*

As an example of Macaulay's ability to sustain a complex narrative, "Samuel Johnson" (1856) is perhaps less impressive than "William Pitt," but it is an excellent essay, which the *Encyclopaedia Britannica* reprinted until 1965. Like other *Encyclopaedia* articles and the essays on Addison and Fanny Burney, "Samuel Johnson" shows that Macaulay's prose style changes. According to Trevelyan, "Macaulay's belief about himself as a writer was that he improved to the last; and the question of the superiority of his later over his earlier manner may securely be staked upon a comparison between the article on Johnson in the *Edinburgh Review* and the article on Johnson in the *Encyclopaedia Britannica*" (II, 371–72). Trevelyan does not elaborate this point, but it is worth exploring since it challenges the received opinion that Macaulay's manner is always the same. Can Trevelyan's claim that his uncle's writing improved be explained by the tendency of Victorian biographers to exaggerate the merits of their subjects? Or does the second Johnson essay differ significantly from the first?

Compared to the early essay on Johnson (1831), the later study reveals (1) a more favorable view of Johnson as a man; (2) sounder critical judgments; and (3) a somewhat less elaborate prose style. These changes must have been apparent to Matthew Arnold, whose disparaging comment on Macaulay's rhetoric was quoted in Chapter 1, because Arnold said that the 1856 biography was written when Macaulay's "style was matured," and he chose Macaulay's second Johnson essay as an introduction to his edition of the *Lives of the Poets*.[1]

If the second Johnson essay is superior to the first, as Trevelyan claims and Arnold implies, one reason may be that an article for the *Encyclopaedia* would naturally be written more carefully than a periodical article. In addition, the Johnson essays fall into different categories, argument and narrative. Although the earlier work contains narrative passages, its intent is to elaborate three points: Croker failed in his attempt to edit Boswell; Boswell was a great fool who wrote a classic; and Johnson united "great powers with low prejudices" (*Works*, VIII, 95). Since the 1831 portrait of Johnson must illustrate the third thesis, it cannot be subtle or convincing. The 1856 sketch, on the other hand, is purely narrative. Given these facts, differences between the works cannot be attributed solely to changes in Macaulay's thought and prose style. But the fact that twenty-five years separate the two Johnson essays suggests that their dissimilarities result more from changes in Macaulay than from their separate aims, to persuade and to inform, or from their places of publication.

The second "Samuel Johnson," like the life of William Pitt, conveys a genuine fondness for its subject, whereas the 1831 review of Croker's Boswell does to Johnson what Macaulay had accused Johnson of doing to Milton: it makes him "the butt of much clumsy ridicule" (VII, 5). Grotesque details used to describe Johnson's appearance in 1831, for example, are not repeated in the second essay. By stressing the idea that poverty, poor health, and a melancholy temperament created Johnson's eccentricities, Macaulay avoids the censorious tone of his 1831 characterization. Moreover, he perceptively describes the influence of Johnson's early years upon his habits and actions as an adult. Macaulay had noted in "Byron" that a writer who relies on startling contrasts to draw a character will produce not a believable human being but a "personified epigram" (VII, 560), and he illustrates this truth himself in his 1831 treatment of Samuel Johnson. The idea that Johnson joined great powers to low prejudices, for example, is variously paraphrased:

> his mind dwindled . . . from gigantic elevation/to dwarfish littleness
> a mind at least as remarkable for narrowness/ as for strength

Through such repetitions, Macaulay conveys no information about the writer but merely a disparaging attitude toward him.

But in the 1856 article, phrases such as the following, which serve both as transitions and as summaries, give Macaulay's narrative a compassionate tone:

> under the influence of his disease
> with such infirmities of mind and body
> the effect of the privations and sufferings
> one hard struggle with poverty
> seven years . . . passed in the drudgery of penning definitions

This later, sympathetic view of Johnson is foreshadowed by a passage in "Madame D'Arblay" in which Macaulay says that he knew Johnson was a benevolent man, "but how gentle and endearing his deportment could be" was revealed only with the publication of Fanny Burney's *Diary and Letters* (X, 23). Since this work appeared after the first essay on Johnson, it may have caused Macaulay to take a more generous view of the writer when he returned to him in 1856.

The critical parts of the 1831 review, like the account of Johnson's character and personality, are superficial, moralistic, and politically biased. The Tory politician John Wilson Croker had infuriated Macaulay by attacking him in Parliament. Croker's edition of Boswell gave Macaulay a chance for revenge. "See whether I do not dust that lying varlet's jacket for him," Macaulay boasted to his sister Hannah; "I detest him more than cold boiled veal" (5 August 1831; Pinney, II, 84). The review is a better gloss on these statements than an evaluation of Croker's work. An able scholar, Croker is as vigorously abused by Macaulay as the hack poet Montgomery had been in an 1830 review. Macaulay ridicules his enemy for minor inaccuracies and gives him no credit for gathering much valuable and curious information or for interviewing people who had known Johnson, whose testimony might have been lost if Croker had not seen the importance of preserving it.

Boswell does not fare much better than Croker: the paradox that he wrote a great book because he was a great fool has become notorious. It is consistent with the primitivistic theories expounded in "Milton," in that it attributes no conscious art to Boswell. Writing twenty-five years later, however, Macaulay, though he still deprecates Boswell's character, no longer considers him a fool. Instead, he describes the process by which the biography was written: having closely studied Johnson, Boswell would turn the talk to subjects likely to draw memorable comments from him and then keep very detailed notes of the conversations. "In this way were gathered the materials, out of which was afterwards constructed the most interesting biographical work in the world" (*Works*, X, 474–75). By using the word "constructed" Macaulay implies that Boswell selected and arranged his material to create a great work.

Although Johnson's works are considered more briefly in 1831 than in 1856, comparison of the treatments gives other evidence that Macaulay's critical judgments were more perceptive in the second work. In 1831, for example, he states that Johnson's "whole code of criticism rested on pure assumption, for which he sometimes quoted a precedent or an authority, but rarely troubled himself to give a reason drawn from the nature of things" (VIII, 101). This emphatic and oversimplified comment—*whole* code/*pure* assumption/*rarely* troubled—typical of Macaulay's early criticism, is easily refuted by Johnson's discussion of the unities in the "Preface to Shakespeare." Equally patronizing is Macaulay's treatment of Johnson's prose style: "All his books are written in a learned language, in a language which nobody hears from his mother or his nurse, in a language in which nobody ever quarrels, or drives bargains, or makes love. . . . He did his sentences out of English into Johnsonese" (VIII, 108). Johnson's natural style of conversation is then sharply contrasted to his "pompous and unbending" written style (108–109).

But Macaulay writes with more detachment and accuracy about Johnson's prose style in 1856, observing that it developed from the early, ornate style, to the "easier and more graceful" language of the *Journey to the Hebrides*, to the "colloquial ease" of the *Lives of the Poets* (X, 478; 483), the work that he considers Johnson's best. The reference to the "colloquial ease" of the *Lives* shows Macaulay abandoning the contrast made in 1831 between Johnson's spoken and written styles. In 1856, he evaluates twelve works by Johnson.

He notes, for example, that some critics praised the style of the *Rambler*, while others condemned it. But the most astute critics, he adds, though finding Johnson's diction sometimes artificial, did justice to his powers of observation, "to the constant precision and frequent brilliancy of his language, to the weighty and magnificent eloquence of many serious passages, and to the solemn yet pleasing humour of some of the lighter papers" (X, 462). Here the mean between extremes attitude characteristic of Macaulay's best writing refines rather than oversimplifies a point. The description of the *Rambler* quoted here shows Macaulay's appreciation of Johnson's prose style, an appreciation that he clearly lacked in 1831.

A difference between the two essays that explains why the second is fairer to Johnson as a man and as a writer is that the 1831 article shows Macaulay's habit of fastening on a single, often arresting answer to a question or a single key to a writer. Thus he says of Johnson in the first essay that "the characteristic peculiarity of his intellect was the union of great powers with low prejudices" (VIII, 94–95). Macaulay's energy is then devoted to expanding and paraphrasing the statement. The pattern could be shown by a dot with many circles around it. In *Edinburgh* essays of the 1840s, however, he does not insist on single explanations. No characteristic feature accounts for the personalities or writings of Fanny Burney or Joseph Addison. Many details build up an impression of Johnson in 1856. Similarly, Bunyan in an early review is judged the only writer who made allegory interesting, but in the 1856 *Encyclopaedia* article a detailed account of his life explains indirectly why the form Bunyan chose suited him so well. The pattern of these later essays is one of interwoven threads.

Thus far the Johnson essays have been sharply contrasted. When prose style is considered, somewhat artificially, apart from the opinions of Macaulay summarized above, the difference between "Samuel Johnson" of 1831 and of 1856 is not as great. Macaulay retains his emphatic manner, as can be seen from passages in the 1856 essay that were toned down or eliminated by Thomas Seccombe in revising it for the eleventh edition of the *Encyclopaedia*. Macaulay described Johnson's friend Levett, for example, as a doctor "who bled and dosed coal heavers and hackney coachmen, and received for fees crusts of bread, bits of bacon, glasses of gin, and sometimes a little copper" (X, 477). Seccombe changed the passage to read that Levett "had a wide practice, but among the very poorest class," an emendation that would have amused Macaulay. Although neither Johnson essay could be mistaken for the work of anyone but Macaulay, because his prose has a characteristic vigor and liveliness, the change from single explanations to more complex accounts of writer's lives and works is naturally reflected in his prose style.

Two comments on Boswell's defects, made in 1831 and 1856, show that the earlier style is the more self-consciously rhetorical. A very long sentence in the first essay begins: "Servile and impertinent, shallow and pedantic, a bigot and a sot, bloated with family pride, and eternally blustering about the dignity of a born gentleman . . ." (VIII, 78–79). Macaulay writes in 1856: "That he was a coxcomb and a bore, weak, vain, pushing, curious, garrulous, was obvious to all who were acquainted with him" (X, 473). In the first example, polysyndeton is used for emphasis:

> servile *and* impertinent
> shallow *and* pedantic
> a bigot *and* a sot.

Macaulay's negative judgment is somewhat milder in the second passage, "weak," "garrulous," "vain," and "curious" having replaced "servile," "bloated," and "eternally blustering."

In 1831 Macaulay characterized Johnson's political writing as "torrents of raving abuse" (VIII, 99), while in 1856 he uses a more specific and less censorious phrase to describe some of the definitions in the famous *Dictionary*: "bitter and contumelious reflections on the Whig party" (X, 467), a phrase worthy of Johnson himself.

Macaulay's tone is more moderate in 1856, as the change from "abuse" to "reflections" illustrates. The use of allusion in two other passages shows a similar change. In 1831 Macaulay alludes to Squire Western as he charges Johnson with excessive party spirit, adding that Johnson was at the same time apathetic about public questions, "a mere Pococurante" (a character in *Candide* whose name means "little-caring"). In 1856 Macaulay says that Johnson did not understand the quarrel with the American colonies well enough to write a successful pamphlet on taxation, but that Edmund Burke might have failed if he had tried to write comedies and that Joshua Reynolds might have been unsuccessful at painting landscapes. Here the allusions are far better suited to a man of Johnson's stature and are drawn, appropriately, from members of his circle. The mention of

Squire Western and Pococurante, while clever, lacks the precision and naturalness of the allusions to Burke and Reynolds.

In each essay, at the point when Johnson goes to London, Macaulay describes the hardships faced by writers in the eighteenth century. The second account (X, 450–51) is far shorter and more concrete than the first (VIII, 85–90), and ends with a vivid little scene that shows a skillful use of contrast: "One of the publishers to whom Johnson applied for employment measured with a scornful eye that athletic though uncouth frame, and exclaimed, 'You had better get a porter's knot,[2] and carry trunks.' Nor was the advice bad; for a porter was likely to be as plentifully fed, and as comfortably lodged, as a poet" (X, 451). Besides the stated contrast of poet-porter, there are implied contrasts between deserved reward for literary talent and its actual reward, between Johnson's appearance and his ability, and between advice that an ordinary man would take and advice that Johnson, a superior man, would take. By reversing the reader's expectation—"nor was the advice bad"—Macaulay stresses the improbability of success for a writer without patrons. The scene also foreshadows Johnson's long struggle with poverty.

Style can be understood not only through a writer's choice of specific devices by also by the way a work is structured. The three-part structure of the 1831 "Samuel Johnson" has already been mentioned. The second essay has two main parts: Johnson's life and work before 1762, the year he received a pension; and his life and work after 1762. But there are other patterns besides the chronological. Johnson's career is more prominent in the first section, his private life in the second.

Since the drama of Johnson's struggle for recognition appealed to Macaulay more than his psychological complexities, Johnson is portrayed as a man contending against great difficulties, especially sickness and poverty. This theme appears at the beginning of the essay when Macaulay lists Johnson's childhood afflictions and adds, "But the force of his mind overcame every impediment" (444). A transitional paragraph in the middle of the essay develops the point: "For the first time since his boyhood he no longer felt the daily goad urging him to the daily toil. He was at liberty, after thiry years of anxiety and drudgery . . . to lie in bed till two in the afternoon, and to sit up talking to four in the morning, without fearing either the printer's devil or the sheriff's officer" (468). This passage restates what has gone before and prepares for what will come: the phrase "since his boyhood" recalls the beginning of the essay; the allusions to toil and the printer's devil remind the reader of circumstances surrounding works Johnson wrote before 1762; "thirty years of anxiety and drudgery" recalls an earlier statement that "this celebrated man was left, at two-and-twenty, to fight his way through the world" (448); "at liberty" suggests Johnson's unsuccessful attempt to win Lord Chesterfield's patronage; and the phrase "to sit up talking" prepares for the description of Johnson's club. The essay ends with the statement that Johnson was "both a great and a good man" (488). The adjectives correspond to the two parts of the essay: the greatness of Johnson is emphasized as he struggles to become a writer (section one), while his goodness is made clear in the account of his private life (section two), especially in a deathbed scene. Macaulay describes the sorrow of Johnson's friends in somber and restrained prose (487).

A metaphor also unifies the second essay. To summarize the introductory paragraphs, Macaulay writes: "The light from heaven shone on him indeed, but not in a direct line, or with its own pure splendour. The rays had to struggle through a disturbing medium; they reached him refracted, dulled and discoloured by the thick gloom which had settled on his soul" (447–48). This light metaphor, with its suggestions of Johnson's greatness and the hardships of his life, epitomizes the essay. Macaulay had written in 1831 that Johnson's mind "was hedged round by an uninterrupted fence of prejudices and superstitions" (VIII, 100), a lively metaphorical thrust but one which, like other statements in the essay, reveals more about Macaulay than about Johnson. The more appropriate summary of the second essay, expressed by light versus darkness, reappears near the end when Johnson finds "his whole life darkened by the shadow of death" (X, 484). Darkness seems to triumph over light. But Macaulay says in the deathbed scene, "When at length the moment, dreaded through so many years, came close, the dark cloud passed away from Johnson's mind. His temper became unusually patient and gentle" (487); the light was no longer refracted by gloom.

Both Johnson's moral and intellectual qualities are implied by the statement that "the light from heaven shone upon him," and the passing of the dark cloud at the end figuratively announces the triumph of his genius over his infirmities. Macaulay's early prose style, with its stark contrasts, shallow paradoxes and overwrought descriptions cannot do justice to the complexity of Johnson. The language of the severe judgments of 1831 shows an inflexibility, an almost Puritanical recoiling from Johnson's excesses. Macaulay's later style, on the other hand, is better suited to his subject. As the Johnson scholar G. B. Hill observed: "In the [1831] essay we seem to look upon the picture of a Tory painted by a Whig. In the life we have the portrait of a great man drawn by another great man."[3]

Trevelyan was justified, therefore, in calling the later essay on Johnson superior to the earlier essay. Whether the works demonstrate that Macaulay's writing "improved to the last" is less certain, for this second claim of Trevelyan assumes a development in Macaulay's prose style. This much is clear: He developed in the sense that as he turned from argumentative writing to narration, he gradually found a form suited to his ideas. The rhetoric of the arguments calls attention to itself, while the rhetoric of the narratives is more subtle. It is unfortunate, therefore, that the 1831 argumentative review is taken to be Macaulay's considered opinion of Johnson. The 1856 biography of Johnson, like the essays on Addison and Pitt, deserves to be better known. These works show Macaulay's narrative art at its best.

### CHAPTER 8

# *The* History of England

MACAULAY considered the *History of England from the Accession of James II* as a far more serious work than his reviews, and the work by which posterity would judge him. The first two volumes were published in 1848. Already famous as an essayist, orator, and Indian legislator, Macaulay then became what he had aimed to be, an eminent historian. He later became a rich one as well: in 1856, a year after the appearance of volumes three and four, his publisher gave him a single check for £20,000. The *History* was so widely read that it was compared to Byron's poems and the novels of Scott. Great and humble Victorians alike recorded their reactions in their diaries and letters; nearly everyone praised Macaulay for having written a lively narrative. But Carlyle wrote in his journal in April 1849 that he found "a very great quantity of rhetorical wind" in the *History*.[1] Macaulay would soon write in *his* journal that Carlyle was "an empty-headed bombastic dunce."[2] The unprecedented success of Macaulay's work must have reminded Carlyle of his very different experience, years of obscurity, relative poverty, and publishers' rejections.

The prestige enjoyed by a best-selling Victorian author is hard for modern readers to appreciate, since writers no longer appear in the guise of sages, as the major Victorian poets and prose writers did. Macaulay was nearly as popular as Dickens, and readers reacted very personally to the historian, as to the novelist. One who was illegitimate, upon finding the word "bastard" in the *History*, called on the author and begged him not to "sanction so cruel an epithet with his immense authority" (Trevelyan, II, 375). After the entire work was read to a group of men by their employer, they voted to thank Macaulay for having written "a history which working men can understand" (*Ibid.*, p. 173). Flattered as he was by praise from

English reviewers and honors from foreign academies, Macaulay was more gratified by such popularity among ordinary readers, because one of his aims was to enlarge the audience for historical writings. To some his popularity proved the shallowness of the work and the readiness of an uncritical audience to adopt a complacent view of English institutions. But the spirit of the *History* is not complacency but exuberant patriotism, and the work would never have achieved its fame if Macaulay had failed to accomplish another of his aims, which was to show that history could be as interesting as fiction.

His original boundaries were the Revolution of 1688 and the 1832 Reform Bill: he had planned "an entire view of all the transactions which took place, between the Revolution which brought the Crown into harmony with the Parliament, and the Revolution which brought the Parliament into harmony with the nation" (*Ibid.*, I, 442). This ambitious design was not realized, however: the *History* covers only seventeen years, from 1685, when James II became king, to 1702, the death of William III. When he studied seventeenth century England, Macaulay had the advantage of experience in Parliament during the second "revolution," when he had been one of the youngest and most influential spokesmen for reform. Thus his emphasis on politics in the *History* resulted from his experience. The defeat of the Whigs in 1841 left him more time to write (he had been secretary at war), and in November of that year he wrote enthusiastically to Napier of the "interest and delight" with which he was pursuing his work, and added: "I really do not think that there is in our literature so great a void as that which I am trying to supply. English history, from 1688 to the French Revolution, is even to educated people almost a terra incognita" (*Ibid.*, II, 52). Although he covered only a fragment of this period, his account of the reigns of James and William is so vivid that his interpretation of late seventeenth century English history changed that era from an unknown territory to a very familiar part of England's past.

Since Macaulay's major work has elicited far more critical response than the essays,[3] treatment of it here will focus on two subjects: his view of history and his way of writing it, as exemplified by a single chapter of the *History of England*. Aside from their intrinsic merit, the essays give a good introduction to the *History*. An early essay gives Macaulay's theory of historical composition, and statements in other *Edinburgh* articles shed light on some ideas embodied in the *History*.

## I  *Conception of History*

The essay titled "History" which appeared in the *Edinburgh Review* in 1828 was ostensibly a review of *The Romance of History* by Henry Neele, but Macaulay mentions neither the author nor his book as he propounds his own view of history. The essay has two parts, a discussion of ancient history that cites specific writers and a more general treatment of modern history. The main points are: (1) history ideally should combine reason and imagination; (2) history is a branch of literature sharing some characteristics with other arts; and (3) history should encompass not only public events and the deeds of the great but also the lives of ordinary people.

Macaulay finds the works of classical historians deficient in analysis (reason) but good as literature (imagination), a dichotomy also expressed by the terms "theory" versus "fiction" and "speculative" versus "narrative," used to describe the contrasting ways in which history has been written. At the beginning of the essay "Hallam," also written in 1828, Macaulay protests that imagination and reason have partitioned the province of history (*Works*, VII, 221). Modern historians are stronger than the ancients in reasoning power—they make better generalizations, for example—but they have neglected the art of narration, Macaulay claims in the essay on history. Neither ancient nor modern work wholly satisfies him, therefore, but taking the strength of each he argues that the ideal history would display both the narrative excellence of classical historians and the analytical power of their modern counterparts. He admits that a writer who combined such different skills would be an "intellectual prodigy" (220). Macaulay was later to praise the Whig historian Sir James Mackintosh for approaching his ideal: Mackintosh's work on the 1688 Revolution exhibits "the diligence, the accuracy, and the judgment of Hallam, united to the vivacity and the colouring of Southey" (VIII, 425). In other words, it is both analytical and imaginative. Macaulay adds that a history of England written in this way would be "the most fascinating book in the language" (425), a remark that foreshadows his attempt to write history according to the theory set forth in 1828.

The importance Macaulay assigns to the art of narration in the essay "History" leads him to consider how historical writing resembles not only other literary genres—fiction, biography, drama— but also painting. Since history is relatively rather than absolutely true, because all details of all events cannot be recorded, careful selection is essential to the historian's art: "Those are the best pictures and the best histories which exhibit such parts of the truth as most nearly produce the effect of the whole" (VII, 177). The historian who seeks to produce the effect of the whole can learn this from painting: "History has its foreground and its background: and it is principally in the management of its perspective that one artist differs from another." Some events require large-scale representation, while others can be condensed; the combined results of events that can be treated only in passing will be indicated by "a few slight touches" (178). The analogy drawn here between painting and the art of historical narrative was recently cited to illustrate that "not only did Macaulay's range of material open up history to artistic treatment, but his methods of writing were consciously esthetic."[4]

Parallels to other art forms are also instructive. Macaulay says that because the historian describes the actions and motives of men, he resembles both the dramatist and the novelist. Readers learn how the Puritans talked from Scott's novels, for example, but such "fragments of truth" should be preserved also by the historian, instead of being scornfully rejected (217). Macaulay cites Boswell's *Life of Johnson* and Southey's *Life of Nelson* to prove that a work may be highly entertaining and popular and at the same time be truthful. But historians have ignored the lively and fascinating details used by Boswell and Southey because, having a false idea of the dignity of history, they confine their accounts to dramatic events such as wars and revolutions; and as a result they miss "the most characteristic and interesting circumstances" of the eras they chronicle.[5] They allow themselves to be hemmed in by meaningless conventions (212). This idea is stressed again in the essay on William Temple: the letters of Temple and his wife, Dorothy Osborne, are intrinsically valuable to the historian for providing the kinds of details not found in government records (IX, 18–21). It is clear from "History" that Macaulay did not consider the artful use of details from private life as ornamental but rather as essential to conveying truth.

He argues, therefore, that the scope of history must be broadened to include "ordinary men as they appear in their ordinary business and their ordinary pleasures" (VII, 215) and thereby to include significant details not found in accounts of heroes or great events. Central to Macaulay's view of history is the theory of "noiseless revolutions":

The circumstances which have most influence on the happiness of mankind, the changes of manners and morals, the transition of communities from poverty to wealth . . . from ferocity to humanity—these are, for the most part, noiseless revolutions. Their progress is rarely indicated by what historians are pleased to call important events. They are not achieved by armies, or enacted by senates. They are sanctioned by no treaties, and recorded in no archives. . . . The upper current of society presents no certain criterion by which we can judge of the direction in which the under current flows. . . . We must remember how small a proportion the good or evil effected by a single statesman can bear to the good or evil of a great social system. (213–14)[6]

This is Macaulay's conception of social history. If the boundaries of history were properly widened to include matters important to ordinary people, an account of the English Reformation, for example, would treat not only Henry VIII but would describe the religious quarrels that divided families (218). As Macaulay sought to bring middle class people into narratives previously devoted largely to the aristocracy, many today seek a further extension to include such groups as the poor, blacks, native Americans, and women. Feminists believe, for example, that the scope of history must be enlarged to include the accomplishments of women thus far "recorded in no archives." But Macaulay himself would not have gone so far. For him "Social history could play the role of social anodyne. Placing really important historical changes into the context of a general moral atmosphere rather than into one of politics and public affairs tended to diminish, or blur over, the significance of contemporary confrontations of rich and poor, progress and reaction, in the political sphere."[7]

Occasionally, however, Macaulay illuminates the conflicting interests of leaders and the people, as, for example, when he observes in the essay on Frederic the Great (1842) that although the Seven Years War enhanced Frederic's reputation, it devastated Prussia: "A sixth of the males capable of bearing arms had actually perished on

the field of battle. . . . The whole social system was deranged"
(*Works*, IX, 642). The characteristic antithesis of a sentence quoted
above—single statesman versus great social system—is suggested
here.

Macaulay's attention to the ordinary Prussian soldiers as well as to
Frederic, illustrating his emphasis on social history, shows his difference from Carlyle, who described history as the biographies of
great men. An early essay by Carlyle reveals, however, that he
agreed with two key points of Macaulay's article: Carlyle urges historians to look beyond public events, and he focuses on the creative
dimension of historical narrative by contrasting the "Artist," who
writes history with an "Idea of the Whole," and the "Artisan," who
merely gives facts. Underlying this distinction between the artist
and the artisan is an antithetical pattern frequently found in Carlyle:
living-good versus mechanical-bad. Echoing Macaulay's statement
on noiseless revolutions, Carlyle in a later essay praises the historical novels of Scott for teaching that "the bygone ages of the world
were actually filled by living men, not by protocols, state-papers,
controversies, and abstractions of men." Carlyle adds that this truth
has been overlooked by historians, a comment very much in the
spirit of Macaulay's "History."[8]

Both Carlyle and Macaulay regarded history as a branch of literature. In a discussion of Macaulay's essay, Sir Charles Firth notes
that modern historians tend to see history as a branch of science
rather than literature; they "enlarge upon the difficulty of finding
out the truth, whereas Macaulay enlarges upon the difficulty of
stating it."[9] This second choice fit Macaulay's temperament; he was
not attuned to uncertainties or inclined to make tentative conclu-
sions.

The main points of his 1828 review are succinctly expressed in a
passage near the end:

The perfect historian is he in whose work the character and spirit of an age is
exhibited in miniature. He relates no fact . . . which is not authenticated
by sufficient testimony. But, by judicious selection, rejection, and arrangement, he gives to truth those attractions which have been usurped by
fiction. In his narrative a due subordination is observed: some transactions
are prominent; others retire. But the scale on which he represents them is
increased or diminished, not according to the dignity of the persons concerned in them, but according to the degree in which they elucidate the
condition of society and the nature of man. (VII, 216)

The first three sentences imply that a combination of reason and imagination is needed by the historian. Macaulay then refers to the importance of skillful narration. Finally, he recommends that the historian look beyond the deeds of the great to understand the past fully.

His insistence of this last point shows the influence of the Romantic movement upon him, and the emphasis on imagination can be traced to the same source. It is clear from the essay "History" that artistic narration is valued for its own sake. Less important is a concern for the teaching function of history, which suggests the moral earnestness associated with the Victorians. If the truths of the past were made vivid and concrete in well-written accounts, Macaulay declares, they would be "not merely traced on the mind, but branded into it" (219–20). Although he claims that a knowledge of the past will help one understand the future, this commonplace is an underlying assumption of the essay rather than an explicitly defended principle. The essay is more appropriately viewed as a sign of the general Romantic rebellion against traditional ways of thinking than as a characteristically Victorian statement.

Macaulay's idea of social history may owe something to Francis Jeffrey, the first *Edinburgh Review* editor, whose work Macaulay greatly admired. Jeffrey wrote in 1808 that the important events in a nation's history result from a change in the "general character" of its people; to trace such a change and its variations is therefore "to describe the true source of events; and, merely to narrate the occurrences to which it gave rise, is to recite a history of actions without intelligible motives, and of effects without assignable causes . . . [The historian must consider] manners, education, prevailing occupations, religion, taste,—and, above all, the distribution of wealth, and the state of prejudice and opinions."[10] Macaulay expresses the same thought through his phrase "noiseless revolutions" and through the distinction he draws between the upper current of society and the under current. Similarly, in the Machiavelli essay, he states that "historians rarely descend to those details from which alone the real state of a community can be collected" (VII, 71), i.e., to the subjects mentioned by Jeffrey—work, manners, religion, popular opinion, and the distribution of wealth. Brief comments in Macaulay's other essays, in speeches, and in journal entries shed more light on his view of history.

Since he thought of history as a cycle of action and reaction, he defends the French Revolution in the following terms: "Demolition is undoubtedly a vulgar task; the highest glory of the statesman is to construct. But there is a time for everything,—a time to set up, and a time to pull down. . . . It is the natural, the almost universal, law, that an age of insurrections and proscriptions shall precede the age of good government, of temperate liberty, and liberal order" ("Mirabeau," *Works*, VIII, 224). The inevitability of this cyclic action is suggested by the allusion to Ecclesiastes 3:1–4. In an example from the *History*, the timely intervention of William III and the strengthening of parliamentary rule saved England from the fate of other countries: chaos, followed by despotism, followed by more chaos (III, 281). In passages describing action and reaction, Macaulay frequently uses process metaphors to make occurrences seem both natural and inevitable; sowing and reaping, for example, become equivalents for historical events.

The gradual movement of the cycle is toward improvement, as suggested in the passage cited above by the transformation from an age of insurrection to an age of order; but regressions can occur, and within short periods, progress cannot always be discerned. In a reform bill speech Macaulay admits that in small segments history can be made to prove "anything, or nothing." Nevertheless, it is "full of useful and precious instruction when we contemplate it in large portions . . ." (XI, 490). One important lesson, clear from a passage in "Mackintosh," is that progress is not confined to material benefits: "The history of England is emphatically the history of progress. . . . [of a] great change in the moral, intellectual, and physical state of the inhabitants of our own island. There is much amusing and instructive episodical matter; but this is the main action" (VIII, 442–43). Macaulay celebrated this main action in his *History of England* (an early description of it appears at the end of "Southey"). But another lesson he draws from history is that even progressive events like the French Revolution bring concomitant evils. Thus his idea of progress is neither simple nor absolute; he did not regard it as a dogma or a universal law of history.[11]

The idea of progress strongly appealed to Macaulay, however, because of his sanguine temperament, not because he placed material values ahead of spiritual values. History showed him that material progress, good in itself, could create moral improvements. Thus when he describes travel conditions in 1685 in the third chapter of the *History*, he says: "Every improvement in the means of locomotion . . . tends to remove national and provincial antipathies, and to bind together all the branches of the great human family" (I, 389), a hypothesis that twentieth century history would seem to demolish, but one that shows the humanitarian side of Macaulay's idea of progress. While the theme of England's increasing material progress is important to the *History*, it should be seen in the light of Macaulay's purpose, to trace the development of English liberty. Ralph Waldo Emerson wrongly concluded that Macaulay "teaches that *good* means good to eat, good to wear, material commodity."[12]

He naturally stresses the Whig role in fostering the development of English liberty. In the seventeenth century, the term "Whig" was associated with Presbyterianism and rebellion, and the term "Tory" with Anglicanism and loyalty to the crown. The Whigs stood for a limited constitutional monarchy, while the Tories favored a divine-right monarchy. In the eighteenth century and during Macaulay's political career, the Whig party was identified with the aristocratic, land-owning families of England and also with the wealthy merchants, for whom laissez-faire was a chief principle of government. Although sometimes taking the side of dissent and reform, notably in the struggle for the passage of the Reform Bill, the Whigs were for the most part opposed to the more radical changes favored by the Utilitarians and the Chartists, for example, universal suffrage. In the first issue of the *Westminister Review* in 1824, the Utilitarian thinker James Mill argued that the English aristocracy had two parties to represent it, the Whigs and the Tories.

Critics who regard Macaulay's *History of England* as a compendium of Whig biases have missed its complexity. The context for Macaulay's Whig views is not a political ideology but is rather an ideal of moderation. He sees the Whigs as the moderate party and thus praises them throughout the essays and speeches. The Whigs uphold a principle defined in the Hallam essay as reform in order to preserve. When Macaulay sums up his interpretation of the 1688 Revolution at the end of volume two, he says, "It is because we had a preserving revolution in the seventeenth century that we have not had a destroying revolution in the nineteenth" (III, 288), a point that seemed especially important in the year 1848 when he wrote this summary. Because the French Revolution was bloody and violent, reform having come too late to preserve, it had the unfortunate effect in England in the first decades of the nineteenth century of hardening resistance to any change and consequently of forcing public opinion into radical and reactionary extremes. Thus Macaulay complained before the Reform Bill was passed: "There are those who will be contented with nothing but demolition; and there are those who shrink from all repair" ("Hallam," VII, 324). The important role of the Whig moderates, in the nineteenth century as in the seventeenth, was therefore to steer a middle course; they were the natural upholders of civil and religious liberty because they were untainted by fanaticism.

At the same time that Macaulay's party bias has been exaggerated, his conception of history has been denigrated. A single sentence from a letter is often quoted to show that his view of history was insufficiently serious. He had written to Napier in November 1841 that he had finally begun his historical research, and he added: "I shall not be satisfied unless I produce something which shall for a few days supersede the last fashionable novel on the tables of young ladies" (Trevelyan, II, 52). Unfortunately for Macaulay's reputation, the statement out of context lends itself to distortion. J. C. Morison, the author of the Macaulay volume of the English Men of Letters series remarks contemptuously, for example, "This, then, was Macaulay's pole-star, by which he guided his historical argosy over the waters of the past—young ladies for readers, laying down the novel of the season to take up his History of England."[13] A modern critic after quoting the same words of Macaulay states: "Thus he deliberately set out to compete with the light novels of his day."[14]

Such judgments are most unfair, as familiarity with the tone of his letters clearly demonstrates. He often wrote in a playful, self-deprecating way, and thus it is likely that this remark to Napier should be seen as a jest; Macaulay pokes fun at his ambitious plan. Behind the remark is an earnest belief that history *could* be made as interesting as fiction, but believing that is far different from seeing his work in the category of light novel. If it is to be taken seriously, Macaulay's letter should be seen in connection with the statement in his 1828 essay that history should reclaim "those attractions which have been usurped by fiction" (*Works*, VII, 216). The ancient historians were good storytellers, and Macaulay wanted to imitate them so that history could regain a strength it once had. Far from being a frivolous innovator, he attempts to restore a tradition. His frequent references to classical writers show, moreover, the seriousness with which he approached his work. He wrote in his journal of Thucydides, for example, "I admire him more than ever. He is the great historian. The others one may hope to match: him, never" (25 November 1848; Trevelyan, II, 181). Macaulay would hardly have considered Thucydides an appropriate model if he were trying to compete with novelists.

Other evidence of his seriousness comes from journal entries in which he refers to the judgment of posterity. He writes, for example, "I have aimed high; I have tried to do something that may be remembered; I have had the year 2000 . . . often in my mind; I have sacrificed nothing to temporary fashions of thought and style" (4 December 1848; *Ibid.*, p. 183). Macaulay has been faulted for sacrificing much to temporary fashions—the Victorian trust in progress, for example,—but these passages should demonstrate the unfairness of attempts to discredit him by plucking one sentence from his letters and using it as a key to the *History of England*.

Macaulay's remark about "the last fashionable novel on the tables of young ladies," quoted much more often than his more serious statements about his work, fits the stereotyped view of him as a complacent, superficial writer. But the essay "History" shows that Macaulay appreciated the great difficulties of historical writing, and journal entries reveal his humility in the face of these difficulties. Despite the unprecedented success of the first two volumes of the *History*, he was never satisfied by his writing. A few years before his death he noted in his journal: "Arrangement and transition are arts which I value much, but which I do not flatter myself I have attained" (1 January 1854; *Ibid.*, p. 305). One month later he exclaimed, "What labor it is to make a tolerable book, and how little readers know how much trouble the ordering of the parts has cost the writer!" (6 February 1854; *Ibid.*). Another entry reads: "I can truly say that I never read again the most popular passages of my own works without painfully feeling how far my execution has fallen short of the standard which is in my mind" (undated; *Ibid.*, p. 381).

The standard in Macaulay's mind in the 1840s and 1850s was the same exacting standard that he had proposed in 1828: historians should rely equally on reason and imagination, should cultivate the art of narration, and should emphasize social history. The most frequently anthologized section of the *History*, the famous third chapter titled "England in 1685," has been recognized as a brilliant example of social history, but other chapters give a better idea of Macaulay's ability to sustain a complex narrative. He had noted in his journal: "To make the narrative flow along as it ought, every part naturally springing from that which precedes . . . is not easy" (15 April 1850; *Ibid.*, p. 211). Focusing on one chapter will allow us to see how its arrangement makes the narrative flow along. Macaulay thinks of a part "springing" from another part because he depicts men in action. "In Macaulay all history is scenic," Gladstone wrote.[15] While this has the authoritative ring of Macaulay's own pronouncements, it is somewhat exaggerated: many memorable passages of the *History* are scenes. But summary passages and sections of analysis are also impressive, and without them the full significance of the scenes would be lost.

## II   *Chapter 9*

Chapter 9 deals with events leading up to and following William's arrival in England, events that culminate in the flight of James (*Works*, III, 1–166).[16] In earlier chapters, misgovernment has weakened support for James. In Chapter 9, the crisis deepens as James responds to intensifying opposition by ruling even more despotically. The result is that William is secretly invited to replace him. But the English situation alone does not influence William, whose larger aim is to form an alliance against France. His success in England is caused not only by his military and diplomatic skills but by the mistakes of James and by good luck: Holland is not invaded by France as William prepares to invade England, for example, and a "Protestant wind" helps William's fleet to land. The complexity of this plot is somewhat disguised by Macaulay's ability to keep the main action moving steadily forward while providing a great quantity of background information. Chapter 9 superbly illustrates the principle of foreground and background that he explained in the history essay.

The plan of the chapter seems casual enough at first glance: Macaulay moves back and forth from James to William, from England to Holland, from the supporters of the king to supporters of the prince, and finally from William's camp in England to the court of James. But closer examination shows that the chapter is arranged to give each main part of the story nearly the same number of pages, eighty-eight for events connected with James and seventy-eight for those relating to William. While varying in length and subject matter, the sections are nearly equal in number, nine for James and eight for William. Macaulay wrote in his journal that he hoped to leave no trace in his pages of the "trouble" the writing of them had caused so that they might "seem to flow as easily as table talk" (28

July 1850; Trevelyan, II, 213). He realized that intention in Chapter 9 by smooth transitions from James to William.

The preceding chapter had ended with a dramatic story, the trial of the seven bishops and their acquittal. To explain why James's attack on the Church of England brought such disasterous results and thus to set the trial into a larger context, Macaulay begins Chapter 9 with an analysis of public opinion. Using a technique he called "declamatory disquisition," he sets forth the opposing arguments on nonresistance urged by those who believed a king should be obeyed regardless of his acts and those who felt that extreme cases justify resistance.[17] The conclusion is that injustice has so weakened attachment to the first position that the second now expresses the national mood. With mild skepticism, Macaulay conjectures that among those who abandoned the doctrine of nonresistance were clergymen "whose sagacity had been sharpened by the imminent danger in which they stood of being turned out of their livings . . . to make room for Papists" (*Works*, III, 4). The subsequent narrative, flowing easily from the account of the new consensus, tells what happened after a Whig delegation asked William to come to England at the head of an army.

The transition between analysis and narrative is accomplished by William's first appearance in the chapter. Recognizing the gravity of the crisis that the intransigence of James has caused, William cries "Now or never" in Latin (10), a detail with which Macaulay favorably characterizes him by suggesting both his resolute spirit and his supranational concerns, two motifs in the *History*. By delaying William's entrance until the state of English public opinion is analyzed, Macaulay can introduce William as a redressor of political and religious grievances, and not as a military adventurer. Macaulay lacked Carlyle's admiration for the military hero, and while he portrays William as an able commander, he is more concerned with military skill as a means to a political end, restoring liberty to England. This emphasis follows a principle defended in 1828: the good or evil brought about by a "great social system" far outweighs the good or evil caused by an individual statesman. As a young man he had written in a review for *Knight's Quarterly* that "the line of demarcation between good and bad men is so faintly marked as often to elude the most careful investigation of those who have the best opportunity for judging." Since this is especially true of public men, he continues, "some doubt must almost always hang over their real dispositions and intentions" (*Works*, XI, 368). While the impartial spirit of this statement is not always apparent in the *History*, Macaulay is more concerned with describing the social system than with judging individuals.

Shifts of focus from James to William represent not a hero-villain interpretation of history but a technique to accomplish the narrative end of clarity. The central characters are juxtaposed so that the strengths of William illuminate the flaws of James. William is resolute and shrewd, James wavering and gullible; William remains calm under pressure, while James is volatile and bad-tempered; William is a brave soldier, James a coward. The leaders do have one thing in common, their adultery, but the sin that blackens James's character is a mere lapse for William, a discrepancy that did not go unnoticed by Victorian readers. Although Macaulay exaggerates the virtues of William and the faults of James, he does not portray a struggle between good and evil forces.

Thus he presents James and William not as isolated individuals shaping history by their personalities but rather as men whose lives show the force of circumstances. In this they are closer to characters in George Eliot's novels than to Carlylean heroes, but William and James are not portrayed with Eliot's subtlety and depth. William appears as an instrument through whom the restoration of English liberty and English Protestantism can be accomplished. "Macaulay sees William as on the side of the future," George Levine correctly states. "James and the Jacobites are the last vestiges of the feudal past."[18] The outcome of the struggle between the two sides is predetermined, therefore, but Macaulay likes to speculate on what might have happened to his characters, as if what did happen was not inevitable. He stresses for example the many obstacles faced by William. The action-reaction pattern makes the movement of the chapter seem inevitable, however: the tyranny of James provokes rebellion and chaos; from these come the enlightened order imposed by William. Macaulay creates a sense of the inevitable partly by word arrangements in the chapter—for example, by opening a paragraph about James with four monosyllables: "And now the King, greatly disturbed . . ." (III, 115). In the last third of the chapter, the sense of an impending crash is heightened by a series of miscalculations made in rapid succession by the king.

If James and William are the "uppercurrent" of the story, to use the terms of the history essay, an impression of the "undercurrent" is conveyed through the summary of arguments for and against resisting a king, illustrated by ballads and popular sayings as well as by political tracts; the hostility of the English to soldiers brought over from Ireland to help James maintain order; the persecution of the Huguenots in France and its impact upon Holland; and the reactions to William's army as it marched through England. We see the interconnections between religion and politics, an important thread in the narrative, as they appeared to ordinary people. The ceremony of burning a pope in effigy is described for example, and alluded to thereafter. The question of Ireland which is naturally tied to seventeenth century politics and religion is more fully treated in Chapter 12, but Macaulay's accounts of anti-Irish sentiment in Chapter 9 throw a strong light on conflicts in his own day.

A more explicit parallel between past and present is drawn when William lands at Torbay. A quiet harbor in 1688, "undisturbed by the bustle either of commerce or of pleasure" it has become "the site of crowded marts and luxurious pavilions" (94). Its population has nearly doubled. While Macaulay delights in mentioning such de-tails, including the statistics, they are not really extraneous; from his point of view, the prosperity of Victorian England has its roots in the revolution that began with William's landing. Allusions to Mon-mouth implicitly contrast his unsuccessful rebellion, described in an earlier chapter, to the triumph of William. Some rumors that circu-lated after William's arrival are noted; for example, that his men were giants wearing bearskins who carried enormous weapons. But the people had good reason to welcome the foreigners: "The most rigid discipline was maintained. . . . [The English] were amazed to see soldiers who never swore at a landlady or took an egg without paying for it" (102), a hint that James is unlucky in having for *his* soldiers a mob of Irish Catholics. Concrete details like the egg are typical of Macaulay's *History*. This passage shows his effort to see great events from the perspective of ordinary people.

The chapter ends with the flight of James, vividly described to stress a point made indirectly throughout the chapter but not explicitly stated until the end: James has shown himself to be both "unkingly and unmanly." "As he passed Lambeth," Macaulay writes, "he flung the Great Seal into the midst of the stream, where, after many months, it was accidentally caught by a fishing net and dragged up" (166). The scene is foreshadowed twenty pages earlier when the people of Newcastle throw a statue of James into the Tyne. By his action, James symbolically gives up his claim to the throne. He also expresses the contempt for English government that his actions in earlier chapters have manifested. The detail of the fishing net suggests that he has brought disgrace to England. The flight scene creates suspense by hinting that chaos may result from the loss of the great seal. Thus the fate of the social system is more important than the defeat of the king.

Although the scene puts James in an unfavorable light, our sympathy for him is aroused at several points in the chapter, for example when the men closest to him, whom we know to be traitors, pledge their loyalty to him (116). Vulnerable and trusting, James is clearly to be pitied in this scene. Later the king finds that Princess Anne has run off with the Churchills. "After all that he had suffered," Macaulay writes, "this affliction forced a cry of misery from his lips. 'God help me,' he said; 'my own children have forsaken me' " (134). Both the phrase "after all that he had suffered," which recalls the earlier action of the chapter, and the emphatic phrase "forced a cry of misery from his lips" gain sympathy for the beleaguered king. Another detail that calls attention to the private life of James is effectively introduced when William, whose feelings are usually hidden, receives a letter from James and reacts emotionally to it. Macaulay speculates on the cause of this emotion: William feels the harshness of the fate "which had placed him in such a situation that he could fulfill his public duties only by breaking through domestic ties," i.e., by attacking the armies of his father-in-law, a neat antithetical summary of Chapter 9 which implies that the fate of James is also harsh.

Judged as a composition, Chapter 9 is a great work. Like the *History* as a whole, however, it is less imposing when considered as an historical account. By taking an inherently dramatic action, the downfall of a king, and heightening the drama, Macaulay imposes too artificial a pattern on his material. Stirred by the colorful spectacle of the past and needing no other spur to write about it, he was not very interested in probing for meaning. Thus he failed to achieve or even to suggest the ideal balance between reason and imagination that his essay recommends. Although he thought of history as "a narrative told reflectively,"[19] the work he wrote cannot be so described. The absence of a deeply reflecting intelligence from the *History of England* is unquestionably a defect, but the importance of this defect depends very much on the temperament of readers. Some will find too little complexity in the ideas and too few challenges to think about the past; others will enjoy the emphasis on action and will be attuned to the moderation and common sense pervading the *History*.[20] Because of its vigorous prose style, the work will probably still attract readers in 2000, the year Macaulay had in mind when he wrote it.

Since issues relating to narrative history are still being debated today, it seems likely that the *History* will be remembered not only as a Victorian document but as one of the best examples of historical narrative. Macaulay's way of projecting himself imaginatively into the past may be relevant, too, as historians extend their investigations to minorities, whose experiences are for the most part "recorded in no archives." To write adequate accounts of such groups as women which have not been much studied in the past, to give an "Idea of the Whole" recommended by Carlyle, historians will have to use their imaginative power. And just as Macaulay turned to broadside ballads for impressions of seventeenth century political opinion, historians of the future, studying for example the impact of the Vietnam war will need to know something of the underground presses, and those who explain the revival of the women's movement will have to read widely in feminist press publications.

Whatever its future reputation or importance, the *History of England from the Accession of James II* is extremely important for its impact upon nineteenth century readers. Its audience included nearly everyone who read at all, both in England and America; it was "the only history of such length and detail that has ever been so widely read."[21] Thus Macaulay made history popular. He did this partly by using the wealthy and politically enlightened nineteenth century as a foil to the seventeenth century and partly by conveying to his readers, despite this Victorian frame of reference, his great love of the past. When he refers in the introduction to the "chequered narrative" that follows (I, 3), Macaulay probably has in mind both the broad meaning of the adjective, diversified, and a narrower meaning, marked with alternative light and shade. The antithetical style that suited this conception of the past made the *History* easy to read, and that was another source of its popularity. Moreover, by describing the "undercurrent" of history as well as the "uppercurrent," the lives of ordinary people and minor actors in the drama of the 1688 Revolution, as well as the fortunes of William and James, Macaulay allowed his middle class audience to feel its importance. As he had tried in the essays on Clive and Hastings to arouse the interest of this audience in the British conquest of India, he tried in his more ambitious work to make late seventeenth century English history seem picturesque and exciting.

### CHAPTER 9

# Speeches

M ACAULAY'S success in any of the roles described thus far—
essayist, Indian administrator, historian—would have made
him famous; and he was, in addition, one of the great parliamentary
speakers of his age. Although it is this combination of talents that
makes him unique, in each case a single gift, the power of expression, accounts for much of his impact. Like the essays, the Minute
on Indian Education, and the *History*, the speeches illustrate the
interaction of experience and a shrewd practical sense with a great
knowledge of the past. Macaulay is less interested in finding simplis-
tic lessons from the past than with seeing in the circumstances of
earlier times the origin of modern institutions and conflicts, so that
he can draw elucidating parallels between past and present. As a
result, the speeches, though necessarily topical, are less dated than
one might expect. The best of them fully exemplify Macaulay's
rhetorical skills.

The speeches fall into three groups: election, ceremonial, and
parliamentary speeches.[1] Only the third group, the largest and most
important, will be considered here. Macaulay's speeches in the
House of Commons were delivered in the years 1830–1833, 1839–
1847, and 1853. He sat in the House of Lords for a short time but
did not speak. In 1853 a bookseller published an unauthorized selection of the speeches that, because of its many inaccuracies, prompted Macaulay to issue a corrected edition in the following year.[2] He
says in the preface that he has published his speeches "in mere
self-defense," without having changed them significantly. He concludes that the speeches may lack literary value but will probably
interest future historians (*Speeches*, pp. xii–xiii). Despite this dis-
claimer, the best of the speeches, including four examined in this
chapter, have considerable literary merit, and would perhaps have
secured Macaulay a modest literary reputation in the twentieth cen-

122

tury even if he had written neither periodical articles nor an ambitious *History of England*.

Just as Macaulay owed none of his political influence to high birth or wealth, he owed none of his oratorical influence to an imposing personal appearance or an impressive delivery. Trevelyan quotes *Blackwood's* description of his uncle as "a little, splay-footed, ugly, dumpling of a fellow, with a mouth from ear to ear" (I, 221). *Fraser's* was hardly more flattering: "Mr. Macaulay is short in stature, round, and with a growing tendency toward aldermanic disproportions. His head has the same rotundity as his body, and seems stuck on it as firmly as a pin-head.[3]" His motions were clumsy, according to the *Times*, and he lacked a well-modulated voice (*Ibid.*, II, 85). Macaulay admitted that his manner was cold but added, "when I *do* warm, I am the most vehement speaker in the House" (*Ibid.*, I, 221). He spoke rapidly and without notes, giving the impression that his speeches were memorized; and he was better at set speeches than at extemporaneous debate. Early in 1852 he refused the offer of a cabinet seat because, he notes in his journal, he wanted to concentrate on the *History*, but also because he was "not a debater" (*Ibid.*, II, 232). Nevertheless, Macaulay enjoyed the reputation of a great speaker: Gladstone later recalled that whenever he began to speak, "it was a summons like a trumpet-call to fill the benches."[4] And Bulwer Lytton wrote that "no man in our age has made a more vivid effect upon an audience."[5] Macaulay was only thirty-one when the usually hostile *Blackwood's* compared him to Burke.[6] The language of the speeches evoked these enthusiastic responses.

## I  *Characteristics*

The speeches shed light on the politics underlying Macaulay's Indian adminstration and his writings. In his second reform speech (5 July 1831), he distinguishes between the "question of right" and the "question of expediency" (*Speeches*, p. 23), defending constitutional change on both grounds. A distinctive feature of the speeches is the way Macaulay alternates between these two questions, sometimes advancing humanitarian arguments and at other times relying on purely utilitarian arguments. This combination of appeals rather than a political philosophy characterizes the speeches. But to a greater extent than the essays or *History*, the speeches show the reforming spirit of Macaulay, which some of his contemporaries mistook for a radical spirit.

Because of his willingness to attack the status quo and his pragmatism, Macaulay can be linked to the Utilitarians. He often seems
more comfortable arguing from expediency rather than principle.
"The business of a Member of Parliament," he told Leeds voters in
1832, "is the pursuit not of speculative truth, but of practical good,"[7]
and illustrated this view in the following year with his great speech
"Government of India" and in 1835 with the Minute on Indian
Education. For Macaulay, expediency has no bad connotations but
represents "practical good."

Thus the theoretical aspect of social, religious, and political questions did not often interest him. Many eloquent passages in the
speeches nevertheless show that his concern for the "question of
right" was very strong. He attacked the Corn Laws, for example,
because the poor found them especially harsh (Speeches, p. 424).
From his very first parliamentary speech, on Jewish disabilities, we
see his concern for oppressed minorities. When Unitarians were
threatened with the loss of their chapels, he argued that it was
extremely important to treat Unitarians justly because they were a
small, uninfluential group (Speeches, pp. 337–38). The civil libertar-
ian side of Macaulay is also evident from a campaign speech in which
he describes the Whigs as: " a party which, though often tainted
with the faults of the age, has always been in advance of the age; a
party which, though guilty of many errors and some crimes, has the
glory of having established our civil and religious liberties on a firm
foundation (Speeches, p. 183). Proud of belonging to the party of
Burke, Macaulay brought to his oratory "all the moral fervor that
was his by inheritance and that he had not been able to bring to the
faith of his father. His reform speeches are secular sermons"[8]

Reform in order to preserve, an idea Macaulay took from Burke
and made one of the chief themes of his essays and History, is a
recurring motif in the speeches as well. A contemporary description
of him as a "great reconciler of the new with the old," one who liked
to reinterpret old laws and ways of thinking and thereby "to restore
their original integrity,"[9] emphasizes the second element in the
doctrine of reform in order to preserve. Macaulay's role as a reconciler was no doubt clearer to his Whig colleagues than to his Tory
opponents, who feared the innovations of Whigs and radicals, but
Macaulay so consistently assumed a moderate stance in parliamentary debates that his fundamental acceptance of the political system
could hardly be challenged.

His moderation, which reflects a desire to find a middle ground between too much change and too little, is a second characteristic of the speeches. This mean between extremes attitude is evident from Macaulay's stand on the People's Charter, a set of demands that polarized opinion in the 1830s and 1840s. He warmly defended one of the six proposals, the secret ballot.[10] But in an 1842 speech on the Charter he opposed universal suffrage, judging it "incompatible with property" (*Speeches*, p. 261), and revealing the paternalistic attitude of both Tories and Whigs toward workers by his claim that they misunderstood their own interests by demanding the vote before they were educated.

The moderate tone of the speeches derives not only from positions taken but also from Macaulay's careful portrayal of himself as a sensible, practical man free of rancorous party spirit. Ethical appeal is thus very important in his speeches, for, as he observes in the biography of William Pitt, "The effect of oratory will always to a great extent depend on the character of the orator" (*Works*, X, 522). Allusions that seem ornamental at first glance often serve to characterize Macaulay favorably. Adam Smith is named reverently in the education speech, for example, to suggest that no unwarranted extension of state power is approved by the speaker.

Macaulay usually makes little direct appeal to the emotions of the audience except in perorations of speeches, when he may refer in heightened language to patriotism, duty, Christian principles, or the glorious past of England. In concluding his defense of Melbourne in 1840, for example, he declares that even if the Whigs are driven from office, their righteous cause will triumph; and he identifies the Whigs of 1840 with Milton and John Locke (*Speeches*, p. 208).

In analyzing the career of Pitt, Macaulay writes that the power of speaking is the greatest asset an English politician can have. But herein lies a weakness of the parliamentary system: "That power may exist, in the highest degree, without judgment, without fortitude, without skill in reading the characters of men or the signs of the times, without any knowledge of the principles of legislation or of political economy, and without any skill in diplomacy . . ." (*Works*, X, 517–18). Since the reform speeches Macaulay delivered in his early thirties made him one of the most famous politicians of his day, the candor of this assessment must be admired. If Carlyle and Mill were better than Macaulay at discerning the "signs of the

times," and if the Victorian novelists saw more deeply into charac-
ter, Macaulay did possess the other qualities named here, as his
Indian career demonstrates. But he would not have been sent to
India if his speeches had not made him known.

Aside from their value as political documents and as examples of
Macaulay's thought and expression, the speeches have additional
significance: they reflect a trend away from rule by aristocrats to rule
by the middle class. Politics in the early nineteenth century and
before was thought to be a suitable hobby for the rich. James Mill
charged in the first issue of the *Westminster Review* that aristocratic
interests were protected by both Whigs and Tories; and he labeled
the Whigs, the party out of office, as "the opposition section of the
aristocracy."[11] But according to an article by John Skelton in
*Fraser's* which was written twenty years after Mill's essay, "the
success achieved by Mr. Macaulay—more remarkable and significant that it was in opposition to the prejudices and remon-
strances of some of the older members of the Whig party, opens the
door to a new and increasing class of public men, who would devote
themselves to politics as the business of their lives, as others give
themselves up to science or to the regular professions."[12] Relying on
talent alone, and sometimes voting against his party, Macaulay became a leading figure in Parliament.

Because he relished the drama of his statesman role in the house
where so many illustrious men had sat, Macaulay conveys in his
speeches, especially in the reform speeches, a sense of momentous
results following from the decisions of his audience. The oratorical
quality of his essays and *History* suggests a belief that writing, like
speaking, is an important public function. It is therefore not surprising that Macaulay's speeches closely resemble his writings, although
the language of the speeches is more concise. Turning to four examples, we see the same adroit handling of controversial issues that,
among the periodical works, is best illustrated by "Gladstone" but
also characterizes "Southey" and "Civil Disabilities of the Jews."

## II  *First Reform Speech (2 March 1831)*

Macaulay addressed the House of Commons several times on the
Reform Bill.[13] His position is best described in the first speech
(Clive and Pinney, pp. 165–80), which advances the following ar-
guments:

1. The Reform Bill is good because it extends political power to
the middle class. (In fact, only a portion of the middle class was

enfranchised, and the significance of the bill is still being debated.)
Macaulay defends reform as a compromise between radical and Tory
extremes that will bring no "violent shock to the institutions of our
country" (167).

2. The Reform Bill is practical. "I rest my opinion on no general
theory of government," Macaulay declares; "I distrust all general
theories of government" (167). Here he seeks to refute one Tory
claim, that cries for reform come from visionaries misled by unsound theories of government.

3. The bill will preserve British institutions. While defending
what he calls "government by property," Macaulay denies that the
present system insures it. Extending the vote will strengthen government by property while ridding the country of government by
"certain detached portions and fragments of property" (170). In this
attack on privilege, the object is again to make the bill seem safe.

4. The bill does not represent a break with tradition. Macaulay
shrewdly turns the Tories' appeals to past wisdom against them by
arguing that their ancestors were wise in that "they legislated for
their own times" (171); politicians of the 1830s should do the same.
Implicit in this declaration is the idea that the 1688 Revolution
culminates in the Reform Bill of 1832. English history as a whole,
Macaulay argues in his next speech, can be interpreted as "the
history of a succession of timely reforms" (*Speeches*, p. 26), a recurring theme in his writings.

5. The bill embodies inevitable changes. In an early allusion to an
idea he later develops, that movements are more important than
leaders, Macaulay tells his audience that they cannot prevent the
changes that have led to debate over reform and should therefore
avoid "a hopeless struggle against the spirit of the age" (Clive and
Pinney, p. 178). In a later speech he returns to this point, arranging
his words to reinforce the meaning: "In peace or in convulsion, by
the law, or in spite of the law, through the Parliament, or over the
Parliament, Reform must be carried. Therefore be content to guide
that movement which you cannot stop" (*Speeches*, p. 81). Macaulay
depends in part on memories of the French Revolution to make this
appeal effective.

6. The Reform Bill is good because public opinion supports it.
Macaulay states tersely, "It is said that the system works well. I
deny it. I deny that a system works well, which the people regard
with aversion" (Clive and Pinney, p. 173). In his second reform
speech Macaulay, probably influenced by Bentham, attacks abuses

in the legal system. Anticipating *Bleak House*, he refers to the "bottomless pit of Chancery" (*Speeches*, p. 28). When he speaks of the people, however, and of public opinion, he clearly means the middle and not the lower class; or he assumes that the interests of the classes are identical.[14] This assumption and the hope that middle class virtues would eventually extend to all levels of society are viewed sympathetically by a political scientist who finds in Macaulay's attitude a Marxist parallel: if the middle class becomes universal, the idea of class will lose its significance. "As with Marxism, after the class emphasis, the final goal is to dissolve class by realizing a utopia of individualism."[15]

A common assumption about Macaulay is that he believed the 1832 bill would make further reform unnecessary. But as early as the ballot speech of 1839 he cautions against viewing the bill with excessive reverence, and he urges that it be amended in an address marking his reelection to Parliament in 1852. He goes a step further in one of his last speeches by stating that the bill would have to be changed soon ("Exclusion of Judges from the House of Commons," 1 June 1853; *Speeches*, p. 536). The Second Reform Bill was not passed until 1867, however.

Except for its conclusion, the first reform speech shows fewer rhetorical flourishes than are common in the essays. But Macaulay's antithetical style is obvious throughout, for example in the statement that the constitution no longer fits England because "while the natural growth of society went on [in the decades before 1832], the artificial polity continued unchanged" (Clive and Pinney, p. 172). The pairing of natural-artificial, already used against Southey and later to appear in the Minute on Indian Education, here distinguishes the Whigs, ready to adapt to what is "natural," from the Tories, who unwisely defend an "artificial" system of government. By such emphatic declarations Macaulay "accomplished in a single speech what six years before he had accomplished with a single article." In 1825, "Milton" made him a famous essayist, while his first reform speech "repeated and extended that earlier success."[16]

### III  *Maynooth (14 April 1845)*

The short speech in which Macaulay defends a proposal to increase the yearly grant to Maynooth, a college in Ireland that trained Roman Catholic priests, is important for two reasons: it shows Macaulay's willingness to take an unpopular stand (one that cost him an election), and it gives a concise account of his opinions on religious toleration, a subject he would treat at length in the *History*. The parts of the speech are a refutation of the opponents' three main arguments and an attack upon Sir Robert Peel, the Tory prime minister, for changing sides on Irish questions. The interest of this attack has been lessened by the passage of time. But Macaulay's arguments on grants to a Catholic institution are still worth considering, although not directly relevant to controversies over support for private schools in the United States because an established church is not involved in the present debate.

Macaulay divides his opponents into three groups: (1) those who object merely to increasing the grant; (2) those who oppose any grant to a religion that teaches error; and (3) those who would give no money to any religion. Beginning with the first, least formidable objection to the Maynooth Bill, Macaulay appeals to common sense. If it is right to give any support to the school, it is right to support it adequately; and the present grant does not. To stress the point, he describes the opulence of Oxford and Cambridge, reminding his audience that they have taken over from Roman Catholics the "splendour and plenty" of these schools (*Speeches*, p. 366). Contrasting humble Maynooth with Oxford and Cambridge, Macaulay shifts attention from the specific proposal to increase Maynooth's grant drastically, from nine thousand pounds to twenty-six thousand pounds.

On the question of truth versus error, Macaulay argues that the question is relative, not absolute, the same strategy used against Gladstone's book on church-state relations. Without denying that the Catholic church teaches error (Macaulay is mindful of his audience), he argues that truth is inevitably mixed with error no matter which religion expounds it:

The constitution of the human mind is such that it is impossible to provide any machinery for the dissemination of truth which shall not, with the truth, disseminate some error. Even those rays which come down to us from the great source of light, pure as they are in themselves, no sooner enter that gross and dark atmosphere in which we dwell than they are so much refracted, discoloured, and obscured, that they too often lead us astray (*Ibid.*, p. 368).

The same image evoked in nearly the same words later appears in the second Johnson essay; such repetitions are frequent enough in

Macaulay to suggest a lack of inventiveness. But in the passage quoted here, allusions to Revelation and to original sin, stressing orthodoxy, illustrate a skillful use of ethical appeal. From the innocent-sounding reflections of this passage, however, Macaulay draws inferences that his Protestant constituents must have found pernicious, for he moves from the generalization about truth and error to this specific question: "Is there no mixture of error in the doctrine taught by the clergy of the Church of England? Is not the whole country at this moment convulsed by disputes as to what the doctrine of the church on some important subjects really is?" (*Ibid.*, p. 370). In other words, if the Tractarians are right, the Evangelicals cannot be right as well.

Although he acknowledges the importance of religious questions in the quoted passage, Macaulay risks offending his Protestant hearers by putting them on a level with Catholics. And the citizens of Edinburgh could not have overlooked a pointed reference to competing schools of theology within the Church of Scotland (*Ibid.*, p. 369) to justify the parallel drawn between truth-error within Catholicism and truth-error within Protestantism. Indeed, the voters came to believe that their distinguished representative "had sold out to Popery."[17]

The third question is taken up briefly: Should any state money go to religion? Probably not, Macaulay admits. His defense is the special circumstance of Ireland, a country having a state church that serves an extremely small percentage of the population. The Catholics thus have greater need of help than the minority Protestants. Moreover, England is guilty of misrule in Ireland, and therefore Parliament should look on the newly increased Maynooth grant as "but a small penalty for a great injustice" (*Ibid.*, p. 373). Often accused of being a narrow Whig, Macaulay here supports a controversial Tory bill. He notes at the end of the speech that his vote may cost him his seat in Parliament, but concludes: "My seat . . . shall never be held by an ignominious tenure; and I am sure that it can never be lost in a more honorable cause" (*Ibid.*, p. 378). For his defense of Irish rights and religious toleration, Macaulay was defeated in the Edinburgh election of 1847. (He had also angered whisky merchants by favoring a higher whisky tax and had offended other local businessmen by treating them curtly when they visited him in London.)[18]

In a number of speeches Macaulay eloquently describes suffering in Ireland and predicts that if Anglo-Irish relations are not improved by enlightened political decisions in his time, strife will continue into the twentieth century.[19] Recent Irish history has unfortunately proven Macaulay right.

### IV  *Ten Hours Bill (22 May 1846)*

In this speech (Clive and Pinney, pp. 193–211), Macaulay supports a bill to limit the factory working day to ten hours for women and children. The bill was controversial because it gave the government power over private business. Factory legislation had been proposed many years earlier by Michael Sadler, Macaulay's Tory opponent in the Leeds election of 1832 (Macaulay represented Leeds after his first seat in the House of Commons was abolished by the Reform Bill). In campaign speeches against Sadler, Macaulay agreed that children should be protected but because of his strong laissez-faire philosophy he dismissed factory laws as "quack medicine."[20]

By the time of the Ten Hours debate in 1846, however, Macaulay, having moved away from the strict laissez-faire doctrines that are stated most emphatically in "Southey," was prepared to support factory legislation. The author of "Southey" shows little concern for the plight of the workers, while the parliamentary speaker declares that factory conditions have left the English laborer ruined in "body and mind by premature and immoderate toil" (211).[21]

The Ten Hours speech has two main parts: in the first, Macaulay defends the principle behind the bill and establishes in the second a precedent for the proposed law. The principle of factory legislation is sound for two reasons, he argues: (1) the state must intervene to protect the health of citizens; (2) the state is also justified in regulating factory hours because public morality must be upheld. Macaulay does not discuss the workers' morals but simply notes that without leisure, workers cannot become educated. By implication, their morals will improve with education. To a modern reader accustomed to protective legislation, the right of government to regulate factories seems obvious, but it was far from obvious to Macaulay's audience. Having justified the principles of state control, Macaulay seeks to establish a precedent so that the Factory Act will not seem radical. He argues therefore that by ancient tradition the number of working days has been limited by the state to six. Thus, arguing by analogy, he shows that regulating hours is as defensible as regulating days. It is an ingenious claim, backed up by the historical examples commonly found in Macaulay's speeches and essays.

Opponents of the bill had claimed that it would keep England from competing successfully with countries in which laborers were required to work seventeen hours each day and could thus produce more than their English counterparts. Macaulay attacks this idea first with a humanitarian appeal and then with a reassuring remark on competition. "Would you treat the free labourer of England like a mere wheel or pulley?" he asks the opposition scornfully (207). He then argues that England has nothing to fear from countries in which workers are abused because in the long run these workers will become inefficient.

The humanitarian appeal is central to the speech in that material values are placed below human welfare. Macaulay explicitly states, for example, that in the factory debate "higher than pecuniary interests are at stake. It concerns the commonwealth that the great body of the people should not live in a way which makes life wretched and short, which enfeebles the body and pollutes the mind" (199). Such sentiments would have been out of place in the review of Southey's *Colloquies*. But in the speech on the Ten Hours Bill, laissez-faire is no longer an absolute good. Macaulay echoes the Book of Common prayer when he defends state intervention by saying "We have done that which we ought not to have done [passed the Corn Laws]. We have left undone that which we ought to have done . . . . We have left unregulated that which we were bound to regulate" (210). Macaulay seldom appeals directly to Christian principles in his speeches but often chooses words or phrases with religious connotations to sanction his positions. The Clapham Sect's moral fervor, typically expressed in biblical language, was often found among those contemporaries of Macaulay who had abandoned both the specific doctrines of their parents and the austerity associated with them.[22]

Aside from the morality of legislation to improve working conditions and as important for Macaulay's case is his belief that the proposed law represents a moderate course. He says: "There is no more important problem in politics than to ascertain the just mean between these two most pernicious extremes [too little legislation and too much], to draw correctly the line which divides those cases in which it is the duty of the State to interfere from those cases in which it is the duty of the State to abstain from interference" (195).

Far different is the language of the Southey review, in which state power is called unnatural. To the extent that all subsequent labor legislation develops from early Victorian reforms, a new era in state regulation begins with the passing of the Ten Hours Bill. Macaulay's speech in its support won *Blackwood's* praise for conveying a "genuine hatred of oppression,"[23] but unfortunately for Macaulay's reputation, the speech is not nearly as well known as the essay on Southey.

## V   *Education (19 April 1847)*

The main issue of this speech (Clive and Pinney, pp. 212–33) is whether education is a private or public concern.[24] The speech has two clearly marked divisions: in the first, Macaulay justifies his support of government intervention in education; in the second, he answers objections to the proposed bill. Part one may be further divided into two sections. Macaulay first argues that education of the people is an essential part of a legitimate duty of government, to protect persons and property. Vividly describing past riots, which he attributes to illiteracy, Macaulay argues that once educated, the lower classes will be less likely to threaten property. The tone here conveys a suspicion of the masses, a fear of their potential unruliness. Macaulay defends education as a kind of soporific. He also suggests that all citizens have a right to education and that it is a good in itself. But the argument that the laborer who has been "taught to find pleasure in the exercise of his intellect" (216) will not destroy machines, set fires, or pull down buildings was a very shrewd one to use in the troubled 1840s, a time of Chartist agitation at home and revolution abroad.

An argument more likely to appeal to a twentieth century audience is then elaborated. Some politicians thought free competition ought to exist in education as it did in trade. "Never was there a more false analogy," Macaulay declares (220). Why? Because education is not solely a private affair: whether a citizen has access to good education is a "matter which concerns his neighbors and the State" (220). Here, as in the speech on factory laws, Macaulay distinguishes between material and nonmaterial needs, urging the propriety of government concern with the latter.

In the second part of the education speech he answers opponents of state support. To the charge that it will cost too much, for example, he replies with an argument often advanced by modern liberals:

the cost of keeping people in prison (or on welfare) is far greater than the cost of training them. Macaulay asserts, "For every pound that you save in education, you will spend five in prosecution, in prisons, in penal settlements" (227). He concludes by accurately predicting that future generations will take for granted the establishment of public schools. By 1870, twenty-three years after this speech, national elementary education was achieved in England.[25] The education speech eloquently defends a democratic principle at a time when many feared the spread of literacy. Macaulay tells in the speech how he accomplished one reform: "When I was Secretary at War it was my duty to bring under Her Majesty's notice the situation of the female children of her soldiers. Many such children accompanied every regiment, and their education was grievously neglected. Her Majesty was graciously pleased to sign a warrant by which a girls' school was attached to each corps" (230–31). In taking seriously the education of young girls Macaulay was clearly ahead of his time.

Like any proponent of change, Macaulay has to persuade his audience by stressing the disadvantages of the status quo when he advocates reform. To accomplish this he relies on his talent for illustrating ideas with specific, concrete, and vividly pictorial language. Linking illiteracy to violence, for example, he evokes scenes of the No Popery riots of 1780: noblemen dragged from their carriages, public buildings destroyed, prisons opened. He cites a survey showing that only fifty of eight thousand inmates of a prison could read and write well. He notes that money could be spent for education which is now used "in hunting and torturing rogues" (216). In a mining district, most children attend no school and those who do find "stench, and noise, and confusion" (217). In another passage Macaulay describes a typical school, "a room crusted with filth, without light, without air, with a heap of fuel in one corner and a brood of chickens in another" (223). Having set forth these bleak details, he ends effectively with a biblical echo: because the people demand change, politicians will soon have to give an account of their "stewardship" (233).

An underlying assumption of the speech is that education will make the people think as Macaulay thinks. Despite this complacency, the speech, because of its strong humanitarianism, helps to correct the stereotyped view of Macaulay as a smug laissez-faire liberal. Although he assumes the role of social critic less frequently than Ruskin, Carlyle, or Arnold, he shows in the education speech, as in others, a clear view of great injustices in England and a readiness to correct them. In 1832 he had called West Indian slavery a "foul blot to this country."[26] Illiteracy in 1847 was another foul blot. Thus G. M. Young rightly concludes that humanism transcends pragmatism in Macaulay's speeches.[27]

Comparing two famous Whig orators who preceded him in the House of Commons, Macaulay writes that Pitt "had less amplitude of mind and less richness of imagination than Burke" (*Works*, X, 521), and the same is true of Macaulay himself. But he was a powerful and influential speaker, and the best of his speeches remain persuasive today.

CHAPTER 10

# *Macaulay's Literary Reputation*

A common theme in Macaulay is the fall of great men. Well suited by temperament and experience to portraying the action of public life, he often emphasized a man's fame so that his subsequent downfall would form a striking contrast. As dramatic as the fall of Clive, of Hastings, or of the younger Pitt in three of Macaulay's best essays, however, is his own fall from a high rank among Victorian writers to relative obscurity today. One sign of his low standing is his exclusion from the 1973 Oxford anthology *Victorian Poetry and Prose*. Another is that bibliographies in the last fifteen years list many more studies of minor Victorian authors than of Macaulay. Fortunately for him, perhaps, even writers of dissertations have ignored his work. If he has not become one of "England's forgotten worthies," he is remembered less as a writer than as a representative Victorian, "a sort of human counterpart to the Great Exhibition."[1]

## I  *Decline*

One reason for Macaulay's eclipse is obvious enough, the reaction against the Victorian period, which has been especially damaging to a writer justly called the "pre-eminent Victorian." A second cause, Macaulay's limitations as a writer, must be acknowledged. But a third, the choice of some of his poorest work for texts and anthologies, while perhaps not as influential as the first two, has undoubtedly prevented readers from regarding him favorably. Fourth, because a few works, including "Milton" and "Bacon," became famous while many more were overlooked, critics have tended to base their generalizations upon only a handful of Macaulay's essays and the familiar passages of the *History of England*. The speeches and the *Encyclopaedia* articles are seldom cited. Finally, since the works of Macaulay have been taken as a key to Victorian attitudes, their intrinsic literary merit has not been stressed.

Hostility to the Victorian period has given way in recent years to more sympathetic estimations, but it is still fashionable to regard Macaulay as the epitome of smugness and complacency. It is true that to a greater extent than the other major Victorian authors he celebrated his age, but his criticisms of British institutions are rarely quoted. Macaulay's optimism was based on his trust in reason, his belief that the past furnishes a model for the present, and his confidence in the middle class. The contrasting attitudes and uncertainties of later generations have made both his sanguine spirit and his authoritative tone seem old-fashioned. Today when we think of historical cycles, we are far less likely to think of inevitable progress and improvement, as Macaulay did, than to think of decline. The modern view of history as a science rather than a branch of literature and the trend toward specialization in the humanities have diminished Macaulay's reputation. In an age when literary critics emphasize the text, his broad treatment of biographical and historical influences on writers seems to preclude respect for his criticism. To borrow the key metaphor from *Sartor Resartus*, while George Eliot and Matthew Arnold have appeared in their modern dress of psychology and existentialism—her novels are praised for their deep insight into character and his poems are valued for their expressions of anguish, isolation, and lost meaning—Macaulay, in his Hebrew old clothes, remains ignored.

Though it has been exaggerated, his lack of depth is a limitation in his work. But he was undoubtedly right in predicting that his clarity would sometimes be mistaken for shallowness: "Many readers give credit for profundity to whatever is obscure, and call all that is perspicuous shallow"[11] (Trevelyan, II, 207). Macaulay's writing is often deceptively simple, his clear presentation hiding problems of selection and arrangement effectively resolved and allowing the reader to forget that what appears self-evident because aptly expressed is in fact a striking insight.

Selections that represent Macaulay in anthologies of Victorian prose give a much better idea of his shallowness than of his perspicuity. The merits of the essays, skillful narration for example, would be more apparent if his last essays were reprinted as often as his first. Everyone who has read some Victorian prose knows that in the essay on Samuel Johnson (1831), Macaulay dismisses Boswell as a fool who produced a great book and subjects Johnson to much obtuse commentary. But few know that twenty-five years later, Macaulay wrote another essay on Johnson that reveals a high regard for him as well as a more restrained prose style. Anthologies of Victorian literature reprint the same works and exclude not only the *Encyclopaedia* articles, of which the second "Johnson" is an example, but the best of the *Edinburgh* essays, including "Gladstone," "Addison," and "Civil Disabilities of the Jews." "Milton" represents Macaulay no more fully than *Northanger Abbey* represents Jane Austen; both are youthful efforts, followed by works of greater sophistication. But *Pride and Prejudice* is universally known, while "William Pitt," Macaulay's last essay, remains an obscure title.

A striking example of the harsh treatment of Macaulay that neglect of his best works has allowed is the entry in the index of Walter Houghton's widely quoted study *The Victorian Frame of Mind* which speaks of Macaulay's "anti-intellectualism . . . his dogmatism and rigidity . . . [and] his worship of force."[2] Some evidence can be found in the essays for the first three of these attitudes, but there is no evidence whatsoever that Macaulay worshiped force.

His memorable pronouncements have become separated from and have obscured the works in which they appear, for example the famous aphorism of the Bacon essay, "An acre in Middlesex is better than a principality in Utopia" (*Works*, VIII, 614). In addition, since a few passages in Macaulay have become very well known, excerpts from works have seemed to represent his thought adequately. Thus his fame has paradoxically been harmful to his reputation. Critics would hesitate to deduce Arnold's theory of poetry from a few paragraphs in an essay or George Eliot's opinion of scholars from her portrait of Casaubon. But Joseph W. Reed censures Macaulay for allegedly denying that biography is an art, with no evidence besides the familiar paradox from the 1831 Johnson essay that Boswell wrote a great book because he was a great fool.[3] Macaulay's statements on biographical writings, on Southey's *Nelson* for example (*Works*, VII, 454), as well as his own practice, disprove the claim that he recognized no art of biography. And the notorious disparagement of Plato in the Bacon essay, which seems foolish out of context and which has been described as "the most dangerous of all the pieces of evidence in the hands of the *advocatus diaboli* to disprove the greatness of Macaulay,"[4] is merely one of several devices used in the essay to

magnify Bacon's achievement. It is not meant to be a serious evaluation of Greek thought.

If excerpts from a few works have seemed satisfactory guides to
Macaulay, it is not surprising that differences among the works have
not been more readily acknowledged. When the forty *Edinburgh
Review* articles are taken en masse to illustrate, in Macaulay's
phrase, "the spirit of the age in miniature," distinctive features of
individual works are lost sight of. Questions of style and structure
have generally not been raised about single essays.

## II  *Victorian Criticism*

No great admirer of his fellow historian, Carlyle described
Macaulay as "a poor Holland House unbeliever with spectacles instead of eyes."[5] But at his death in 1859, Macaulay seemed assured
of a very high place in English literature. The mayor of Leicester no
doubt expressed popular sentiment when he said in a speech to the
local literary and philosophical society that Macaulay would rank
with Addison and Johnson. His peroration, a good example of imitation Macaulay, shows how influential the famous style had become:
"Centuries hence, the pages which bear the impress of that fertile
genius will, as now, be read with undiminished interest by the
dwellers in crowded cities and lonely solitudes, under climates the
most various, and in lands the farthest apart; still guiding to high
thoughts, and inculcating generous sentiments; still investing severe truth with more than the charm of the most romantic fiction . . . .[6]" A very different prediction was made a few years later
by Matthew Arnold, who declared that "beyond the apparent
rhetorical truth of things [Macaulay] could never penetrate . . . and
therefore his reputation, brilliant as it is, is not secure."[7] One may
take issue with the first part of Arnold's statement, but the truth of
the second part has been borne out. Seventeen years after
Macaulay's death, when the great popularity of his writings was not
as astonishing as it had been in the 1840s and 1850s, reviewers of
G. O. Trevelyan's *Life and Letters of Lord Macaulay* (1876) could look
dispassionately upon the essayist and historian.

Trevelyan's biography of his uncle, widely praised when it appeared, has always been considered one of the best Victorian lives.
Though not as candid as Froude's *Carlyle,* it is free of both the
unctuous tone of many Victorian lives and their blurred distinction
between biography and hagiography. Gladstone did not complain of

Trevelyan's work, as he later did (according to a popular Victorian anecdote) of the John Cross biography of George Eliot, that it was not a life at all but a reticence in three volumes. The details of Macaulay's private life were especially interesting to Victorian readers, who knew the public man but discovered only with Trevelyan's *Life* that Macaulay was unusually devoted to his family, and they to him. Trevelyan portrays Macaulay as generous (he gave away much of the fortune his books brought him), high-principled, and industrious, but also as extremely fun-loving and witty. If the critics unanimously agreed on Trevelyan's merits as a writer, however, they were less sure of Macaulay's. They found much to applaud, but they also raised what were to become the standard objections to Macaulay.

He is praised for his common sense, his love of liberty, his narrative skill, and his ability to reach a wide audience. The word "manly" recurs as a tribute to him. An underlying theme of the reviews, which frequently appears in twentieth century studies, is that Macaulay's gifts as a prose stylist compensate for his weakness as a thinker. But certain features of the prose were said to reflect flaws in the man. For example, reviewers claimed that Macaulay's writing shows no trace of growth or development; it is poorly suited to analysis; and it is sometimes artificial. The judgment that Macaulay is the voice of his age was less favorable in 1876 than it had been during his lifetime, and it became by the 1920s and 1930s a solid rebuke to the writer.

Assessments of Macaulay by Walter Bagehot, J. A. Froude, Leslie Stephen, John Morley, and W. E. Gladstone, especially the last two show the high quality of Victorian periodical criticism.[8] Unfortunately for Macaulay's literary reputation, the author of a much less able review of Trevelyan, James Cotter Morison, later wrote the Macaulay volume for the English Men of Letters series. An admirer of Carlyle, Morison was not likely to be an admirer of Macaulay as well. His book offers some good commentary but is weakened by narrow, moralistic criticism. Such judgments as the following, more severe in tone than judgments from reviews of Trevelyan, could hardly have enhanced Macaulay's reputation: his writing has had little influence; it lacks moral insight and ethical depth; his intellectual deficiencies are so apparent that no defense of him can be imagined; some of his essays are "thin, crude, perfunctory and valueless"; and finally, Macaulay "has little to say either to the mind or the heart."[9] In 1882, the same year that Morison's book was published, a less comprehensive but more perceptive study appeared in France, *Les Essais de Lord Macaulay* by Paul Oursel. This book comes closer to Arnold's ideal of disinterested criticism than the work of Morison. Oursel examines the form of the essays, not merely their content; suggests that Macaulay's style developed; and identifies the best of the periodical essays, including the articles on Mackintosh, Addison, Gladstone, and Jewish disabilities. Oursel looks favorably upon the practical turn of Macaulay's mind, often cited as a weakness by English critics: he distinguishes pragmatism from mere expediency. And Macaulay's moderate spirit is praised by Oursel, who defends him against the charge of vituperative reviewing by the claim that the tone of English reviews, vigorous and energetic to the point of fierceness (*rudesse*), simply reflects one trait of the Anglo-Saxon race.[10]

### III  *Twentieth Century Criticism*

The same knowledge of individual works shown by Oursel is demonstrated by the great classical scholar R. C. Jebb in a speech at Cambridge in 1900, Macaulay's centenary. Jebb's reprinted speech is not widely known but remains one of the best studies of Macaulay. One reason his estimate seems more favorable than that of other critics, Victorian and modern, is that, like Oursel, he focuses on the works instead of using the works to judge the man; he sees Macaulay's writing as intrinsically valuable. Moreover, Jebb raises several key points either overlooked or insufficiently stressed by earlier critics: (1) the great difference between Macaulay's best *Edinburgh* articles and his worst; (2) his contribution to the historical essay—"These essays are probably the best of their kind in Europe;" and (3) the excellence of the *Encyclopaedia* works—"As a writer of short biographies, Macaulay has not been surpassed, if he has been equalled, by any English writer."

Equally valuable for understanding Macaulay are two other comments by Jebb: short excepts do not give a fair impression of a writer's style, and style should not be considered in the abstract but in relation to a writer's purpose and subject. On the first point, Jebb argues: "As an orator must be judged by a completed utterance, so Macaulay must be judged by large integral units of his composition, such as whole chapters or essays. Both the critics and the imitators of his style have frequently failed to perceive this." It is important to observe that in Macaulay "incidental use of rhetoric is subordinate to a higher energy and a larger inspiration which informs his style as a whole." Since anthologies reprint excerpts as often as "integral units of composition" to represent Macaulay, the distinction Jebb makes between "incidental use of rhetoric" and "style as a whole" has been blurred. Secondly, Jebb defends Macaulay's style against Matthew Arnold's charge, quoted in Chapter 1, that it lacks the "soft play of life." Prose that exhibits the writer's personality should have this quality, but besides subjective styles there are objective styles, of which Macaulay's is a good example. "It suited his subjects," Jebb concludes. It is a formal, public style "especially adapted to the historical presentation of facts."[11] To some extent, Macaulay's reputation has suffered because the works that have become best known, such as "Milton" and "Bacon," furnish some proof for Arnold's claim, while the later and more subtle writings such as "William Pitt," which clearly support Jebb's point about an objective style suited to historical subjects, are seldom read.

Jebb's commentary has not been followed by works of equal merit, for as the editors of the best Macaulay anthology noted in 1972, Macaulay criticism for the most part is "a mere repetition of things that were being said of him in the generation after his death and which have never been reconsidered since."[12] A tendency of some Victorian and modern criticism of the *History*, for example, is to elevate it by dismissing the essays as insignificant pieces. Thus Lord Acton cautioned Mary Gladstone that "the essays are only pleasant reading, and a key to half the prejudices of our age," while the *History* is a great work.[13] Macaulay wished to be remembered as an historian rather than an essayist and referred to his *Edinburgh* articles as "ephemeral." But taken as a whole the essays are far more important than Acton suggests; and the best of them, the narrative essays, more closely resemble the *History* that Macaulay's dismissive label would indicate. Hostile critics have argued, on the other hand, that Macaulay's major work is not really history at all. John Wilson Croker, for example, called it "Mr. Macaulay's historical novel" and a "species of *carnival* history."[14] A more common view is that the *History of England* is a great narrative work but one that lacks "the ballast of central controlling ideas."[15] This dichotomy is suggested by Herbert Butterfield's remark that literary historians, including Macaulay tend to be "too pre-occupied with the mere surface of things."[16] But Jebb defends the *History* in this way: "It may be granted that Macaulay would have been a still greater historian than he is, if he had possessed more aptitude for speculative thought,—if his mind had been more philosophic; but the fact that he was not a philosopher is no reason for denying that he was, in his own way, a great historian."[17]

It is interesting that Jebb does not refer to Macaulay's powerful style to defend him here, but points instead to the question of degree underlying the judgment that the *History* is deficient in analysis. If he had been more philosophic, if he had been a great speculative thinker, he would not have been the same author, Jebb suggests. One may note, too, that pejorative comments on Macaulay's ideas can be translated into a more neutral-sounding evaluation: in the *History*, as in the essays and speeches, Macaulay more often appeals to common sense than to abstract principles. And many sections in the *History* show that he could be adept at analyzing, at getting beneath the surface of things, for example the beginning of Chapter 9 in which he expatiates upon differing views of nonresistance.

Assessments of Macaulay from 1900 to 1920 were generally less harsh than those of the 1920s and 1930s. His reputation seemed to reach a low point with the publication in 1938 of R. C. Beatty's *Lord Macaulay, Victorian Liberal*. This biography was well received by critics, who shared Beatty's patronizing view of the Victorians in general and Macaulay in particular. Perhaps the debunking spirit of Lytton Strachey was still influential in 1938. In any case, a "Southern Agrarian view of Macaulay"[18] and an incomplete grasp of the Victorian age prevent the biographer from making his subject attractive, and Beatty's suggestion that the Whig liberalism espoused by Macaulay led to World War I cannot have encouraged readers to take a sympathetic view of the writer.

The one hundredth anniversary of Macaulay's death in 1959 renewed interest in him, and essays and pamphlets published in that year show more favorable views of Macaulay than were common before 1959. Nevertheless, he remained neglected. Although perceptive essays were published in 1968 by George Levine and William Madden, Macaulay's claim to serious attention was firmly reestablished only with the appearance in 1973 of Clive's *Macaulay: the Shaping of the Historian*, a widely praised work that combines biography and intellectual history. Clive gives the first comprehensive account of Macaulay's relationship to his father, his intense love for his sisters, the various influences upon his writing including Utilitarianism and Evangelicalism, and his career in India. Equally valuable are the discussions of some individual works. "What Macaulay did," Clive concludes, "was to infuse the liberal creed with the spacious and sanguine spirit of humanism and history"[19]

Unfortunately for his literary reputation, Macaulay's humanism has been virtually ignored, but it is convincingly demonstrated by Clive's book. This work restores Macaulay to an honorable place among English writers, and the recent studies by Jane Millgate and Joseph Hamburger should also help to win Macaulay new readers; but he will probably never again be as famous as he was in his own day. If, as criticism in the 1970s suggests, condescending treatments of Macaulay are no longer fashionable, he may be seen to rank among the greatest English prose writers, with Addison and Johnson, the subjects of two of his finest essays.

CHAPTER 11

# Conclusion

W ITH its certainties about this life and the next set forth in elaborate prose, the world of Macaulay's Clapham boyhood seems remote from our own time. But that world seems less distant when we consider the recently awakened interest in Bloomsbury writers and some links between Bloomsbury and Clapham. "Bloomsbury, like Clapham, was a coterie," Noel Annan has remarked. Although the fourth generation of the Clapham Sect abandoned the moral code of their forebears, "one can still see the old Evangelical ferment at work [in the Bloomsbury circle], a strong suspicion of the worldly-wise, an unalterable emphasis on personal salvation and a penchant for meditation and communion among intimate friends."[1] Among the Macaulays' neighbors in the first years of the nineteenth century were the family of James Stephen, grandfather of Virginia Woolf, whose works modern feminists have found so illuminating, and the Henry Thorntons, whose youngest daughter, Laura, was the grandmother of E. M. Forster, who died as recently as 1970. Although the gulf between the pieties of Zachary Macaulay's *Christian Observer* and the sexual revelations of such works as Forster's posthumously published *Maurice* and Nigel Nicolson's *Portrait of a Marriage* is great enough to suggest a pointed contrast of the kind Thomas Macaulay enjoyed making, Forster's life of his great aunt, *Marianne Thornton*, which he subtitles "a domestic biography," presents such an appealing picture of a Victorian family that we can easily and unselfconsciously enter the world of his characters.

Lytton Strachey's *Eminent Victorians* reminds us, however, that the Bloomsbury circle saw itself as wholly different from the Victorians. Strachey, for example, in an arch phrase, described Macaulay's style as "one of the most remarkable products of the Industrial Revolution."[2] And in the preface to his dissertation on

145

Warren Hastings, Strachey termed Macaulay's study of the Indian governor "a masterpiece of imagination, and not of history."[3] Yet in several ways the portraits of Cardinal Manning, Dr. Arnold, Florence Nightingale, and General Gordon that make up *Eminent Victorians* resemble the historical essays of Macaulay. Strachey, like Macaulay, is a rationalist. He emphasizes the public lives of his subjects, as Macaulay did, and is especially drawn to men of action. Seeing his characters from the outside, he has limited insight into their motives and lacks a sense of character developing. Like Macaulay, Strachey chooses vivid details and anecdotes to tell his story, and digresses skillfully. Biographical sketches by Forster and Woolf have a conversational manner, but Strachey's is more formal. Balanced sentences, emphatic phrases, and a studied elegance are some characteristics of his style. Like Macaulay, he alternates very long sentences with short, abrupt sentences and moves with great ease from one topic to the next. Finally, Strachey resembles Macaulay in his love of pointed antithesis, which he often relies on for satirical effect. In the Manning essay, for example, he describes the pope's secretary as a man who "could make innuendoes as naturally as an ordinary man makes statements of fact"; and when the secretary goes mad, Strachey reports that he was "unfortunately obliged to exchange his apartment in the Vatican for a private lunatic asylum,"[4] a line that Macaulay, with his keen sense of the unexpected and the improbable, would have enjoyed.

Macaulay has more in common with another twentieth century writer, George Orwell: both are essayists concerned with literature and politics who served the British Empire in the East, Macaulay in India and Orwell in Burma. Both the writer who helped rule India in the 1830s and the writer who fought with an anarchist brigade in the Spanish Civil War in the 1930s are great champions of civil liberty. Orwell places such importance on the individual that despite his socialism (an idiosyncratic socialism), he fits into the tradition of nineteenth century liberalism that Macaulay represents. In his patriotism, his love of the past, and his moderation, Orwell closely resembles Macaulay, although he has a greater mistrust of imperialism, and favors more fundamental social change than Macaulay would have accepted. But like Macaulay he occasionally tells his readers that they are better off than their ancestors. He describes nineteenth century London slums, for example, in the manner of Macaulay recounting in the third chapter of the *History of England* the harsh life of the seventeenth century. More importantly, Orwell echoes one of Macaulay's favorite themes: the success of the English in creating revolutionary change without bloodshed.[5]

Orwell's essays reveal a special love of the Victorian period, and their didactic strain, softer than Macaulay's, links them to an earlier age than the 1930s and 1940s. Orwell believes in reason, decency, and common sense. Assuming as Macaulay does the air of the plain man, he speaks to a broad middle class audience whose practical outlook he shares, although he is more aware than Macaulay of its limitations. An allusion by Orwell to "smuggy mysticism" shows the untheoretical attitude common to the two writers, an attitude shown also by the way they liken the intangible to the physical and concrete. In arguing for new words to improve the English language, for example, Orwell states that they should be invented as deliberately as new parts for car engines.[6] In addition, the characters in Orwell's novels, like those in Macaulay's *History* and narrative essays, are all one dimensional.

At the beginning of "Politics and the English Language," one of his best essays, Orwell suggests a difference between the romantic and the classical spirit when he contrasts the view that language is a "natural growth" to the view that language is an "instrument which we shape for our own purposes."[7] It is clear from Orwell's defense of the second position that he shared with Macaulay the classical ideals of order and control. Both Orwell's thesis ("If you simplify your English you are freed from the worst follies of orthodoxy") and his prose style show that for him, as for Macaulay, the essential feature of good writing is clarity. Although obscurity in writing lacks for Macaulay the sinister political implications Orwell attaches to it, his comment in the essay on Machiavelli that obscurity and affectation are the worst faults of style (*Works*, VII, 108) is supported by "Politics and the English Language." Compared to other nineteenth and twentieth century writers, neither Orwell nor Macaulay has received much critical attention, and one reason may be that by writing as clearly as they did, they left few puzzles for critics to explain.

It is useful to see what Macaulay has in common with twentieth century writers as different from each other as Lytton Strachey and George Orwell because great emphasis has been placed on his archetypally Victorian character. In some significant ways, however, Macaulay stands apart from his contemporaries. Many of them were highly self-conscious writers in a way he was not, for example. They saw themselves as living in an age of transition, a Victorian theme absent from his writings. His work shows to some degree the Victorian curiosity about process, but studying the present through historical analogies prevented him from fully grasping the significance of the idea, its implications not only for material prosperity but for ways of thinking as well. When he took up contemporary problems in speeches and essays, he applied to them reason and the lessons of the past, not fearing that these might be inadequate. Thus the mood of doubt found in many Victorian poems and prose works is not conveyed by Macaulay. His formal, unemotional style reflects one side of Victorian literature, its public side, but Macaulay differs from many Victorian writers in not using himself as a subject. He is atypical in another important way, too, for he was largely indifferent to religion in an age when both private and public life were strongly influenced by it.

Macaulay lacks some of the gifts of other major Victorian prose writers. The subtlety of Newman, the great penetration into human motives and actions of George Eliot, Mill's freedom from biases of his age, Carlyle's poetic intensity are missing in his writings. He is a great stylist, but certain effects he rarely achieves—for example, the metaphorical brilliance of Carlyle; or the ironic, playful tone of Arnold's essays; or the delicate beauty of a Ruskin work like "Of Kings' Treasuries." But what Macaulay does best, historical narration, he does incomparably well.

Although the Victorian belief in progress is easily illustrated from "Locksley Hall" or the utopian socialism of Morris, or Arnold's belief that poetry would replace religion, Macaulay's writings have seemed a preeminent example of the idea, perhaps because Macaulay describes progress so emphatically and because everything he wrote was so widely read. Yet when his works are taken as a whole, the concept of progress is less central a theme than liberty. The connection between them is that of means to an end: material welfare is good itself but is chiefly valuable for extending human freedom. The humanitarian spirit of Henry Thornton, William Wilberforce, Zachary Macaulay, and their Clapham circle, stripped of piety, animates the speeches, essays, and *History* of the younger Macaulay. He was drawn to the late seventeenth century because he saw it as a time when liberty flourished. He thought the struggles for reform described by the *History* extended to his own period, however, and that is partly why many of his speeches and essays are fiery polemics. He rejected the claim of the aristocracy to be the natural rulers of England, but also believed that "institutions purely democratic must, sooner or later, destroy liberty, or civilisation, or both."[8] The defense of liberty could be entrusted to the middle class, however. Thus the middle class becomes the mean between extremes characteristically sought by Macaulay. His praise of it should be seen in this context.

If, when he extols the middle class and dwells on the wonders of technology, Macaulay seems remote from us, other topics bring him closer. When he judges the workings of social systems to be more important than the acts of heroes; when he worries that Indians will be exploited by his countrymen, predicts that if the Irish question is not resolved in his time it will haunt the twentieth century, and suggests that American institutions will be severely tested in the twentieth century; when he remarks that the debate between science and religion will not be won by appeals to authority; and when he scoffs at James Mill's opinion that women need not vote because their interests are identical to those of their husbands, he sounds very much like our contemporary. "Is the interest of a Chinese the same with that of the woman whom he harnesses to his plough?" asks Macaulay in his best hectoring manner. "Is the interest of an Italian the same with that of the daughter whom he devotes to God?" asks Macaulay the staunch Protestant. But Mill must be answered more emphatically:

Women have always been, and still are, over the greater part of the globe, humble companions, playthings, captives, menials, beasts of burden. Except in a few happy and highly civilised communities, they are strictly in a state of personal slavery. Even in those countries where they are best treated, the laws are generally unfavourable to them, with respect to almost all the points in which they are most deeply interested. ("Mill on Government," *Works*, VII, 354)

By a "highly civilised community" Macaulay of course means England, but the passage shows an awareness of one of its shortcomings.

Thus he can write exuberantly of English progress in "Southey" but attack an unjust law in "Civil Disabilities of the Jews." Similar threads run through his speeches, in which he sometimes defends the status quo and sometimes attacks it. The Minute on Indian Education displays both Macaulay's sense of racial superiority and his eagerness to improve the condition of the Indian people. While accepting, with reservations, the idea of an established church, he can argue that the legitimacy of the state does not come from religion. His patriotism, typically thought of as narrow but often connected to his reforming zeal, takes an appealing form when he praises the great men of England, including Clive, Addison, and Johnson.

Macaulay is most impressive when his major work, the *History of England*, is read in its entirety and its design comprehended. Readers today, however, are more likely to read a fragment of the *History* or some of the essays. The best of these display, on a small scale, Macaulay's great narrative power. But the major shortcoming of his prose, lack of subtlety, is more apparent in extracts and in short works than it is when the *History* is taken as a whole.

Macaulay wrote essays over a long period, from the early 1820s to his death in 1859. Most of the early essays are arguments, while the later mainly narrative essays were written in the 1840s and 1850s, at the same time that Macaulay worked on the *History*. There is some truth to Strachey's remark that the flaws of Macaulay disappear or change to virtues in the narrative works—"narrowness becomes clarity, crudity turns into force"[9]—but Strachey, like Macaulay, exaggerates. Some of Macaulay's arguments, "Civil Disabilities of the Jews," for example, and "Gladstone," neither narrow nor crude, are among the best polemics of the Victorian period. But on the whole the narratives are more effective. As we have seen, the best of them, including the essays on Clive, Addison, and Johnson, have a complexity of execution if not of interpretation.

Macaulay's prose is uniformly vigorous and high-spirited, but the language of the early essays, marked by sharp contrasts, flashy paradoxes, and heavy emphasis, obscures the fact that Macaulay is basically a moderate. His later style, more concise and restrained, is better suited to expressing moderate ideas; and moderation is more typical of the essays considered as a whole than the Whiggism commonly associated with his name. To understand what "liberal" means for Macaulay, it is necessary to remember that the word derives from the Latin for "free" and that among its meanings are free from prejudice and free from an unthinking preference for traditional ideas or institutions. In this sense, "liberal" denotes an attitude rather than a political philosophy. And it is more fruitful to stress attitudes than ideas with Macaulay because, for example, his

belief in laissez-faire and progress, always fastened on by texts and
anthologies, is relevant to only a few of his essays, while his moderate stance characterizes them all.

Even though we do not accept many of the assumptions behind
Macaulay's works or share his optimism, we can enjoy reading him
today because, although he does not often move us deeply, he is
always capable of "surprising, delighting, and instructing [us] by the
felicity of a phrase or the shrewdness of an observation"[10]

We can also appreciate the wonderfully sharp eye for the ludicrous that we find in the pages of Macaulay. Another reason for
reading him today is that he enthusiastically communicates to us, as
to his *Edinburgh* readers, his intense love of literature. And
Macaulay has a rarer gift, the power to describe the past so that it
seems, in T. S. Eliot's phrase, not dead but already living. His
imaginative sense of the past and his immense reading would not
have made his works memorable, however, if he had not also been a
great stylist. Historian, essayist, orator, Macaulay can be read with
pleasure today because of his vigorous style.

Like two other great prose writers whose historian he became,
Addison and Johnson, Macaulay was buried in Westminster Abbey.
To the twentieth century, he has seemed more a monument than an
attractive or accessible figure, very different from the writer whom
two young girls in 1850 were delighted to spot at the zoo: "Is that
Mr. Macaulay? Never mind the hippopotamous" (Trevelyan, II,
191). The value of his *History*, essays, and speeches as "signs of the
times" has always been recognized, but some of his best writing has
been neglected. By examining the characteristics of individual
works, this study has attempted to show that Macaulay wrote much
that is valuable in itself, apart from its value as a key to an age.

# Notes and References

## Chapter One

1. *The Times* (London), 10 January 1860, p. 8.

2. The statement that "every schoolboy knows who imprisoned Montezuma, and who strangled Atahualpa" appears at the beginning of the Clive essay, *The Works of Lord Macaulay*, 12 vols. (London, 1898), IX, 186. Subsequent references to this standard edition, the Albany edition, will be made in the text.

3. George Otto Trevelyan, *The Life and Letters of Lord Macaulay*, 2 vols. (1876; rpt. Oxford, 1961), I, 56. The standard biography, Trevelyan's work was first published in 1876. It will be cited hereafter in the text.

4. For Scott's influence see Hugh Trevor-Roper, *The Romantic Movement and the Study of History* (London, 1969), pp. 16–21; and "Sir Walter Scott and History," *Listener* LXXXVI (August 1971), 225–32. See also Jane Millgate, *Macaulay* (London, 1973), pp. 120–21. The importance of the castle building habit is discussed by John Clive in "Macaulay's Historical Imagination," *Review of English Literature*, I (October 1960), 20–28. See also Trevelyan, I, 170–71.

5. In the introduction to *Thomas Babington Macaulay, Selected Writings* (Chicago, 1972), John Clive and Thomas Pinney distinguish between the "controversial and the descriptive" essays (p. xv). Quotations from several works will be taken from the Clive and Pinney anthology because it is more accessible than the Albany edition. Page references will be in the text. William Madden classifies Macaulay's prose works by three styles, which he terms "oratorical," "judicious," and "histrionic." See "Macaulay's Style," in *The Art of Victorian Prose*, eds. George Levine and William Madden (New York, 1968), p. 134.

6. *The Letters of Thomas Babington Macaulay*, ed. Thomas Pinney (London, 1974), II, 110. Three volumes of this definitive edition have appeared, covering the years 1807 to 1841. Subsequent references to Pinney will be made in the text. Letters written after 1841 will be quoted from Trevelyan.

7. The most important of these is Clive's monumental work *Macaulay:*

*the Shaping of the Historian* (New York, 1973). See also the excellent appraisal by Millgate, and Joseph Hamburger's *Macaulay and the Whig Tradition* (Chicago, 1976).

    8. S. C. Roberts titled a pamphlet "Macaulay: the Preeminent Victorian" (London, 1927).

    9. Clive, *Macaulay*, p. 94.

    10. *The Diary of Crabb Robinson, an Abridgement*, ed. Derek Hudson (London, 1967), p. 93.

    11. Quoted by Frederick Arnold, *The Public Life of Lord Macaulay* (London, 1862), p. 118. Arnold includes Macaulay letters that are less flattering to him than those in Trevelyan.

    12. John Morley, "Macaulay," in *Nineteenth Century Essays*, ed. Peter Stansky (Chicago, 1970), p. 83.

    13. *Ibid.*, p. 77.

    14. R. C. Jebb, *Macaulay* (Cambridge, 1900), p. 49.

    15. Matthew Arnold, *Friendship's Garland*, 2nd ed. (London, 1897), p. 71. See also "Joubert," in *The Complete Prose Works of Matthew Arnold*, ed. R. H. Super (Ann Arbor, 1960—), vol. III, *Lectures and Essays in Criticism* (1962), 210.

    16. E. M. Forster, *Marianne Thornton* (New York, 1956), p. 56.

    17. When Macaulay judged Bunyan's allegory more interesting than Spenser's, he added for emphasis: "Very few and very weary are those who are in at the death of the Blatant Beast" (*Works*, VII, 608). But the Blatant Beast does not die in the *Faerie Queene*. Macaulay's exaggeration won him a place in Henry B. Wheatley's *Literary Blunders* (London, 1893), pp. 38–39.

*Chapter Two*

    1. "The West Indies" rather than "Milton" was Macaulay's first *Edinburgh* work. See Jane Millgate, "Father and Son: Macaulay's *Edinburgh* Debut," *Review of English Studies*, XXI (1970), 159–67. "The Present Administration," the two antislavery articles, and "The London University" are omitted from collected editions of Macaulay's works. Clive and Pinney reprint "The London University" in their anthology.

    2. "The Present Administration," *Edinburgh Review*, XLVI (1827), 247.

    3. John MacCunn, "Macaulay the Reforming Whig," *Proceedings of the Literary and Philosophical Society of Liverpool*, 60 (1907), 1.

    4. "The Present Administration," p. 262.

    5. Gertrude Himmelfarb, *Victorian Minds* (New York, 1968), p. 289.

    6. J. S. Mill, *Autobiography* (London, 1873), p. 158. See also pp. 157–61.

    7. James Anthony Froude, "Reynard the Fox," in *Short Studies on Great Subjects* (London, 1882), I, 603–604.

    8. See Clive's analysis of the essay, *Macaulay*, pp. 106–109.

9. This is the main theme of Joseph Hamburger's cogent study, *Macaulay and the Whig Tradition* (Chicago, 1976).
10. Review of Trevelyan's *Life and Letters of Lord Macaulay, Quarterly Review*, CXLII (1876), 19.
11. For a modern view of Southey's book and Macaulay's attack upon it see Martin Jarrett-Kerr, "Southey's *Colloquies*," *Nineteenth Century and After*, CXXXII (1942), 181–87.
12. John Holloway, *The Victorian Sage. Studies in Argument* (London, 1953).
13. Charles Dickens, *Hard Times* (London, 1854), p. 10. In his journal, Macaulay labeled the novel "sullen socialism," adding that he preferred Austen to Dickens (Trevelyan, II, 307).
14. Israel Abrahams and S. Levy, eds., *Essay and Speech on Jewish Disabilities by Lord Macaulay*, 2nd ed. (Edinburgh, 1910), pp. 11–12. The speech reprinted here and also in Clive and Pinney was delivered in 1833, but Macaulay's first parliamentary speech, 5 April 1830, also dealt with the Jewish question. For background see Albert Hyamson, *A History of the Jews in England* (London, 1908), pp. 319–26.
15. Abrahams and Levy, pp. 69–70.
16. Robert Smith, "The New Captivity of the Jews," *International Review of Missions*, XXX (1941), 225–31.
17. John Robertson, "The Macaulay Election of 1846," *Quarterly Review*, LXXXI (1847), 539.

### Chapter Three

1. The possibility that Macaulay had incestuous feelings for his two youngest sisters is judiciously considered in chapter ten of Clive's *Macaulay*. The incest question has been raised more recently by reviewers of Pinney's edition of Macaulay's letters. See for example J. H. Plumb, "Writing to Someone," *New Statesman*, 12 July 1974, pp. 51–52.
2. See also Gerald Sirkin and Natalie Sirkin, "The Battle of Indian Education: Macaulay's Opening Salvo," *Victorian Studies*, XIV (1971), 407–28; and R. K. Das Gupta, "Macaulay's Writings on India," in *Historians of India, Pakistan and Ceylon*, ed. C. H. Philips (London, 1961), pp. 230–40. Useful background is provided by Eric Stokes in *The English Utilitarians in India* (Oxford, 1959) and in "Macaulay: The Indian Years," *Review of English Literature*, I (1960), 41–50.
3. Clive, *Macaulay*, p. 360.
4. In an introductory note to the Minute, Clive and Pinney state (p. 237) that "the correctness of these policies [favoring English] is still being argued about today, but there is no doubt that their consequences for India were immense." The arguments are described in Chapter 13 of Clive's *Macaulay*.
5. Max Warren, "The Church Militant Abroad: Victorian Missionaries,"

in *The Victorian Crisis of Faith*, ed. Anthony Symondson (London, 1970), p. 67.

6. Clive, *Macaulay*, p. 367.

7. Sirkin and Sirkin, p. 418.

8. Clive, *Macaulay*, p. 388.

9. "Government of India," 24 June 1853, *Hansard's Parliamentary Debates*, 3rd series, CXXVIII (1853), 759.

10. For Macaulay's later opinions, see the summary of the 1847 education speech in Chapter 9.

11. For an analysis of the Minute, see Clive, *Macaulay*, pp. 369–76.

12. In essays observing Macaulay's centenary, however, two Indian writers treat his Minute very sympathetically: C. D. Narasimhaiah, "Thomas Babington Macaulay," *The Literary Criterion*, Mysore, IV (1959), 56–64; and K. R. Srinivasa Iyengar, "Thomas Babington Macaulay," *The Aryan Path*, XXX (1959), 551–52.

13. See Clive, *Macaulay*, Chapter 14. The code was not enacted until 1862, three years after Macaulay's death.

14. David Kopf, *British Orientalism and the Bengal Renaissance* (Berkeley, 1969), p. 244. See also pp. 245–51.

15. Undated minute on the Black Act of 1836 in C. D. Dharker, ed., *Lord Macaulay's Legislative Minutes* (London, 1946), pp. 177–78.

*Chapter Four*

1. For an excellent analysis of "Bacon" see Clive, *Macaulay*, pp. 483–91.

2. Letter from Calcutta, 1 January 1836, *Selection from the Correspondence of the Late Macvey Napier*, ed. Macvey Napier, Jr. (London, 1879), p. 174. This work includes Macaulay letters not in Trevelyan and letters referring to Macaulay by Jeffrey, Brougham, and others.

3. See Millgate, *Macaulay*, pp. 82–92, for a perceptive commentary on the Temple essay.

4. See Madden (p. 137) on the "judicious" style of the Gladstone essay.

5. G. M. Young, *Early Victorian England* (London, 1934), II, 458. The speech on the Ten Hours Bill is discussed in Chapter 9.

6. This phrase, which I have borrowed for "Southey," was used by S. C. Roberts (p. 12) to describe the third chapter of the *History of England*.

7. Quoted by John Morley in *The Life of William Ewart Gladstone* (London, 1903), I, 305.

8. Hippolyte Taine, *History of English Literature*, trans. H. Van Laun (London, 1880), IV, 237.

9. W.E. Gladstone, "A Chapter of Autobiography," in *Gleanings of Past Years* (New York, n.d.), VII, 151, 145–48, 137. Gladstone's letter to Macaulay and Macaulay's reply are reprinted here, pp. 106–108.

10. Paul Oursel, *Les Essais de Lord Macaulay* (Paris, 1882), p. 106.

## Chapter Five

1. This edition omits seventeen of the *Edinburgh Review* articles.

2. Trevelyan said Macaulay was "probably the worst electioneer since Coriolanus" (II, 245). He angered Edinburgh voters by supporting Maynooth, a Catholic college in Ireland. His Maynooth speech is summarized in Chapter 9.

3. For Macaulay's connection to the famous Whig center of Holland House, see Clive, *Macaulay*, Chapter 8.

4. 9 February 1841; Napier, p. 344.

5. Cf. this passage from *Areopagitica:* "I cannot praise a fugitive and cloister'd vertue, unexercis'd & unbreath'd, that never sallies out and sees her adversary . . . ." *Complete Prose Works of John Milton*, ed. Don M. Wolfe (New Haven, 1953–1971), vol. 2, ed. Ernest Sirluck (1959), p. 515.

6. Macaulay mentions the revisions in a letter dated 27 August 1844; Napier, p. 470.

7. Plutarch, *Eight Great Lives*. The Dryden translation revised by Arthur Hugh Clough, ed. Charles Alexander Robinson, Jr. (New York, 1960), p. 184.

8. Robert Southey, *Life of Nelson* (London, 1813), I, 1.

9. William Minto, "Macaulay," in *Manual of English Prose Literature* (Boston, 1887), p. 104.

10. An exception is a fine commentary by Jane Millgate in *Macaulay*, pp. 92–97. She notes that analogies in the essay, the conquest of Mexico likened to that of India, for example, depend "as much upon emotional as upon intellectual responses" (p. 96).

## Chapter Six

1. Lois Whitney, *Primitivism and the Idea of Progress* (Baltimore, 1934).

2. See P. L. Carver, "The Sources of Macaulay's Essay on Milton," *Review of English Studies*, VI (1930), 49–62; and Frederick L. Jones, "Macaulay's Theory of Poetry in Milton," *Modern Language Quarterly*, XIII (1953), 356–62. More recently, Terry Otten has cited Jeffrey but argued against tracing the theory to a single writer. See "Macaulay's Secondhand Theory of Poetry," *South Atlantic Quarterly*, LXXII (Spring 1973), 280–94. For a more general and rather unsympathetic account of Macaulay's literary opinions see René Wellek, *A History of Modern Literary Criticism 1750–1950* (New Haven, 1965), III, 125–31. See also George Levine, *The Boundaries of Fiction* (Princeton, 1968), pp. 103–108.

3. Quoted by Leslie Stephen, *The English Utilitarians* (London, 1900), II, 363.

4. For an analysis of "Milton" as an argument, one of very few studies that explicates a single work of Macaulay, see Martin J. Svaglic, "Classical

Rhetoric and Victorian Prose," in *The Art of Victorian Prose*, eds. George Levine and William Madden (New York, 1968), pp. 273–86.

5. Joyce Hemlow, *The History of Fanny Burney* (Oxford, 1958), pp. 459–60.

6. J. W. Croker, Review of *The Diary and Letters of Madame D'Arblay*, *Quarterly Review*, LXX (June 1842), 243–87.

7. "Observations on Novel Reading," *The Christian Observer*, XV (1816), 784–87.

8. Henry James, *The Question of our Speech. Balzac. Two Lectures* (Boston, 1905), p. 62.

9. "The Function of Criticism at the Present Time," in *The Complete Prose Works of Matthew Arnold*, III, 283.

10. Austin Dobson, *Fanny Burney* (New York, 1903), p. 202.

11. Virginia Woolf, *The Common Reader* (London, 1925), p. 132; p. 139.

12. *Ibid.*, pp. 132–33.

13. Pinney, I, x.

14. See Donald F. Bond, ed., *The Spectator* (Oxford, 1965), I, ciii-civ; and Peter Smithers, *The Life of Joseph Addison*, 2nd ed. (Oxford, 1968), p. vii.

### Chapter Seven

1. *The Six Chief Lives from Johnson's Lives of the Poets, with Macaulay's Life of Johnson* (London, 1878), p. xxv.

2. Porter's knot: "A kind of double shoulder-pad, with a loop passing round the forehead, the whole roughly resembling a horse-collar, used by London market-porters for carrying their burdens." (O.E.D., V, 742).

3. G. B. Hill, *Dr. Johnson: his Friends and his Critics* (London, 1878), p. 97.

### Chapter Eight

1. James Anthony Froude, *Thomas Carlyle: A History of his Life in London* (New York, 1884), I, 385–86.

2. This opinion, from Macaulay's unpublished journals at Trinity College, Cambridge, is quoted by R. C. Beatty, "Macaulay and Carlyle," *Philological Quarterly*, XVIII (1939), 32.

3. See especially Sir Charles Firth, *A Commentary on Macaulay's History of England* (London, 1938; rpt. 1964). Clive does not treat the *History* directly, but *Macaulay: the Shaping of the Historian* is essential for an understanding of the work. Millgate devotes three chapters of her *Macaulay* to the *History*. Hamburger treats the *History* in chapter four of *Macaulay and the Whig tradition*. See also Levine; Mark A. Thomson, *Macaulay*, The Historical Association pamphlet No. 42 (London, 1959);

Peter Gay, *Style in History* (New York, 1974); and H. R. Trevor-Roper's introduction to an abridged edition of the *History* (New York, 1968). Clive and Pinney summarize criticism of the *History* in the Macaulay chapter of *Victorian Prose: a Guide to Research*, ed. David J. DeLaura (New York, 1973), pp. 27–30.

    4. Avrom Fleishman, *The English Historical Novel* (Baltimore, 1971), pp. 134–35.

    5. For Macaulay's stress on circumstances, see Clive, *Macaulay*, pp. 119–23.

    6. Cf. this sentence from "Mitford's History of Greece," a review that appeared in *Knight's Quarterly* for 1824: "The happiness of the many commonly depends on causes independent of victories or defeats, of revolutions or restorations,—causes which can be regulated by no laws, and which are recorded in no archives" (*Works*, XI, 389–90).

    7. Clive, *Macaulay*, p. 123.

    8. See the beginning of *Heroes and Hero-Worship* for the description of history as the biographies of great men. The contrast between the Artist and the Artisan appears in "Thoughts on History," *Fraser's Magazine*, II (1830), 416. Carlyle's remarks on Scott are quoted by Trevor-Roper, *The Romantic Movement*, pp. 23–24.

    9. Firth, pp. 28–29.

    10. Francis Jeffrey, Review of Fox's *History of James II*, *Edinburgh Review*, XII (1808), 284.

    11. G. M. Trevelyan, "Macaulay and the Sense of Optimism," in *Ideas and Beliefs of the Victorians* (London, 1949), p. 51.

    12. Ralph Waldo Emerson, *English Traits*, ed. Howard Mumford Jones (Cambridge, Mass., 1966), p. 159.

    13. James Cotter Morison, *Macaulay*, English Men of Letters (London, 1882), p. 162. Herbert Paul calls Morison's interpretation of Macaulay's letter "nonsense," adding that Gibbon boasted in his *Autobiography* of seeing his history on the tables of young ladies; but no one supposes that Gibbon sought to compete with the author of The *Castle of Otranto*. "Macaulay and his Critics," in *Men and Letters* (London, 1901), p. 305. Morison is attacked on the same point in a review by A. V. Dicey, *Nation*, XXXVI (1883), 195.

    14. Lionel Angus-Butterworth, *Ten Master Historians* (Aberdeen, 1961), p. 109. The author attributes some disparaging remarks about Macaulay to "the German critic Arminius" (p. 110), who is in fact a whimsical creation of Matthew Arnold. Arminius, Baron von Thunder-ten-Tronckh, appears in *Friendship's Garland*.

    15. W. E. Gladstone, Review of Trevelyan's *Life*, *Quarterly Review*, CXLII (1876), 48.

    16. Clive and Pinney include part of this chapter in their anthology *Macaulay, Selected Writings* and briefly describe it in the introduction, pp. xxv–xxvi.

17. Gay, p. 112.
18. Levine, p. 141.
19. D. H. Macgregor, *Lord Macaulay* (London, 1901), p. 67.
20. For a fuller summary of the *History*, see Millgate, *Macaulay*, pp. 179–81.
21. G. M. Trevelyan, p. 47.

### Chapter Nine

1. There is no complete edition of Macaulay's speeches. Most of the twenty-nine works reprinted in *Speeches of the Right Honorable T. B. Macaulay Corrected by Himself* (London, 1854) are parliamentary speeches. This edition will be cited hereafter in the text, except for speeches reprinted in the Clive and Pinney anthology. *Hansard's Parliamentary Debates* includes sixty-four speeches by Macaulay, of which twenty-seven are reprinted in the Albany edition of his works. Excerpts from nonparliamentary speeches can be found in Arnold's *The Public Life of Lord Macaulay.*
2. The bookseller, Henry Vizetelly, gives his side of this affair in *Glances Back Through Seventy Years: Autobiographical and Other Reminiscences* (London, 1893), I, 385–87. For accounts of the speeches see Clive, *Macaulay*, Chapters 6 and 7; and Margaret L. Wood, "Lord Macaulay, Parliamentary Speaker: his Leading Ideas," *Quarterly Journal of Speech*, XLIV (December 1958), 375–84.
3. John Skelton, "Contemporary Orators," *Fraser's*, XXXIII (1846), 83. On Macaulay's rapid manner of speaking Skelton adds, "You think of an express train which does not stop even at the chief stations" (p. 84).
4. W. E. Gladstone, "Macaulay," in *Gleanings from Past Years*, II, 270. Gladstone had originally written simply "a summons to fill the benches." *Quarterly Review*, CXLII (1876), 4.
5. This comment is made in a note to the poem "St. Stephen's," *Lord Lytton's Miscellaneous Works* (London, 1875), VII, 193.
6. "Noctes Ambrosianae" No. LVII, *Blackwood's*, XXX (1831), 410.
7. Quoted by F. Arnold, p. 118.
8. Clive, *Macaulay*, p. 166. Millgate suggests that fervor for the Whig party was a substitute for religion. *Macaulay*, p. 57.
9. Skelton, p. 81.
10. "The Ballot," 18 June 1839, *Hansard's Parliamentary Debates*, 3rd series, XLVIII, 462–76.
11. James Mill, "Periodical Literature," *Westminster Review*, I (1824), 219. The essay is reprinted in *The Emergence of Victorian Consciousness*, ed. George Levine (New York, 1967).
12. Skelton, p. 80.
13. The most complete account of Macaulay's stand on Reform is in

Clive, *Macaulay*, Chapters 6 and 7. See also Hamburger, and G. O. Trevelyan, Chapter 4.

14. For good discussions of this question see Clive, *Macaulay*, pp. 168–70; and MacCunn, pp. 14–17.

15. Vincent E. Starzinger, *Middlingness: Juste Milieu Political Theory in France and England, 1815–48* (Charlottesville, Va., 1965), p. 70.

16. Clive, *Macaulay*, p. 162.

17. R. C. Beatty, *Lord Macaulay, Victorian Liberal* (Norman, 1938), p. 291.

18. *Ibid.*, p. 292. Macaulay was also accused of giving up his independence by taking a cabinet post, a charge he answers in a campaign speech reprinted in F. Arnold, pp. 311–15.

19. For Macaulay's treatment of Ireland in the *History of England*, see Chapter 8 of Millgate's *Macaulay*.

20. See F. Arnold, p. 141. See also pp. 98, 106, and 125.

21. Cf. the blunter language of Engels: "Simply in order to fill the pockets of the bourgeoisie, women are rendered unfit to bear children, children are crippled, while grown men are stunted and maimed." *The Condition of the Working Classes in England*, tr. W. O. Henderson and W. H. Chaloner (Oxford, 1958), p. 188.

22. Macaulay's view of Clapham austerity is suggested by a letter to his sister in which he claims that their father, Zachary, judged "smoking, eating underdone meat, liking high game, lying late in a morning, and all things which give pleasure to others and none to himself to be absolute sins" (30 July 1831; Pinney, *Letters*, II, 81).

23. *Blackwood's*, LXXV (1854), 202.

24. See the introduction to this speech in E. P. J. Corbett, *Classical Rhetoric and the Modern Student* (New York, 1965), p. 313.

25. Clive and Pinney, p. 212.

26. "Slavery in the Colonies," 24 May 1832, *Hansard*, 3rd series, XIII, 55.

27. G. M. Young, in *Speeches by Lord Macaulay with his Minute on Indian Education*, The World's Classics (London, 1935), p. xvi.

*Chapter Ten*

1. The first phrase is the title of an essay on Elizabethan seamen written in 1852 by James Anthony Froude: "England's Forgotten Worthies," in *Short Studies on Great Subjects*, selected by David Ogg (Ithaca, N.Y., 1963). The second phrase is from John Clive, "Macaulay, History, and the Historians," *History Today*, IX (1959), 830. Macaulay heartily approved of the Great Exhibition and visited it often. Carlyle, on the other hand, declared, "I had no idea till late times what a bottomless fund of darkness

there is in the human animal, especially when congregated in masses, and set to build Crystal Palaces . . ." J. A. Froude, *Thomas Carlyle: A History of His Life in London*, II, 70.

2. Walter Houghton, *The Victorian Frame of Mind* (New Haven, 1957), p. 457.

3. Joseph W. Reed, *English Biography in the Early Nineteenth Century*, 1801–1838 (New Haven, 1966), pp. 66–67; 72.

4. W. P. Ker, "Macaulay," in *English Prose*, ed. Henry Craik (London, 1896), V, 415.

5. Froude, *Carlyle*, I, 165.

6. J. F. Hollings, *Lord Macaulay: a Lecture* (London, 1860), p. 55.

7. Matthew Arnold, "Joubert," in *The Complete Prose Works of Matthew Arnold*, ed. Super, III, 210.

8. These essays are listed in the bibliography.

9. Morison, *Macaulay*: little influence, p. 58; moral insight, p. 40; ethical depth, p. 53; no defense, p. 49; perfunctory and valueless, p. 129; and mind or heart, p. 185.

10. Oursel, pp. 129; 98.

11. Jebb: best and worst essay, p. 41; best of their kind, p. 43; short biographies, p. 44; large integral units, p. 48; incidental use of rhetoric, p. 49; objective styles, suited his subjects, historical presentation, pp. 53–54.

12. John Clive and Thomas Pinney, eds. *Macaulay, Selected Writings*, p. x.

13. *Letters of Lord Acton to Mary Gladstone*. 2nd ed. (London, 1913), p. 139.

14. John Wilson Croker, Review of the *History of England*, Vols. I and II, *Quarterly Review*, LXXXIV (1849), pp. 553; 630.

15. Macgregor, p. 91.

16. Herbert Butterfield, *History and Human Relations* (London, 1951), p. 250.

17. Jebb, p. 16.

18. John Clive and Thomas Pinney, "Thomas Babington Macaulay," in *Victorian Prose: a Guide to Research*, ed. David J. DeLaura (New York, 1973), p. 21.

19. Clive, *Macaulay*, p. 497.

*Chapter Eleven*

1. Noel Annan, *Leslie Stephen* (London, 1951), pp. 123; 126.

2. Lytton Strachey, "Macaulay," in *Portraits in Miniature* (New York, 1931), pp. 45–46.

3. Quoted by Michael Holroyd, *Lytton Strachey* (London, 1967), I, 229.

4. Lytton Strachey, *Eminent Victorians* (London, 1918), p. 62. In the

essay on General Gordon, Strachey describes Gladstone as "the rising hope of the stern and unbending Tories" (p. 272), a phrase taken from Macaulay's essay on Gladstone.

5. "The English People," in *The Collected Essays, Journalism and Letters of George Orwell*, eds. Sonia Orwell and Ian Angus (London, 1968), III, 30–31. For the Victorian slum, see III, 57.

6. *Ibid.*, II, 7.

7. *Ibid.*, IV, 127.

8. Letter from Macaulay to H. S. Randall, 23 May 1857, published in "What Did Macaulay Say About America?" *New York Public Library Bulletin*, XXIX (1925), 478.

9. Strachey, *Portraits in Miniature*, pp. 175–76.

10. Clive, *Macaulay*, p. 104.

# Selected Bibliography

PRIMARY SOURCES

The only collected edition of Macaulay, which contains most but not all of his writing, was edited by his sister, Lady Trevelyan: *The Works of Lord Macaulay*. 8 vols. London: Longman, 1866. This edition was reprinted as the Albany edition (12 vols.) in 1898. The first collection of the essays was *Critical and Historical Essays, Contributed to the Edinburgh Review*. 3 vols. London: Longman, 1843. Some essays excluded from this edition are reprinted in *Miscellaneous Writings of Lord Macaulay*. Ed. T. F. Ellis. 2 vols. London: Longman, 1860. Ellis, Macaulay's best friend, wrote an introduction to this work. No edition reprints all of Macaulay's *Edinburgh* essays, but all of them are listed in *The Wellesley Index to Victorian Periodicals*. Ed. Walter Houghton. Toronto: University of Toronto Press, 1966. The five essays Macaulay contributed to the eighth edition of the *Encyclopaedia Britannica* are collected in *Biographies of Lord Macaulay*. Edinburgh: Black, 1860.

The first two volumes of the *History of England from the Accession of James II* appeared in 1848, and the third and fourth volumes in 1855. The last volume was posthumously published in 1861. An edition of the *History* carefully revised by Macaulay was published by Longman in 1858.

There is no complete collection of the speeches. Twenty-nine were reprinted in *Speeches of the Right Honorable T. B. Macaulay, M. P., Corrected by Himself*. London: Longman, 1854; and twenty in a World's Classics edition, *Speeches by Lord Macaulay*. Ed. G. M. Young. London: Oxford University Press, 1935.

Selections from his Indian minutes were published in *Lord Macaulay's Legislative Minutes*. Ed. C. C. Dharker. Madras: Oxford University Press, 1946.

The first two volumes of the definitive edition of Macaulay's letters, edited by Thomas Pinney, were published by Cambridge University Press in 1974, and volume three was published in 1976. Letters through August 1841 are included. Pinney's excellent introduction tells how G. O. Trevelyan (see below) changed some of the letters he published. Some letters after 1841 not in Trevelyan can be found in *Selection from the Correspondence of Macvey Napier*, Ed. Macvey Napier, Jr. London: Macmillan, 1879.

The best anthology, edited by Thomas Pinney and John Clive, is *Thomas Babington Macaulay: Selected Writings*. Chicago: University of Chicago Press, 1972. Other anthologies are those of G. M. Young, *Macaulay: Prose and Poetry*. Cambridge: Harvard University Press, 1967; and Hugh Trevor-Roper, *Critical and Historical Essays, Thomas Babington, Lord Macaulay*. New York: McGraw-Hill, 1965.

SECONDARY SOURCES

1. Bibliographies

BRYANT, ARTHUR. *Macaulay*. London: Peter Davis, 1932. Pp. 172–84. Good short biography.

CLIVE, JOHN, AND THOMAS PINNEY, EDS. *Thomas Babington Macaulay: Selected Writings*. Chicago: University of Chicago Press, 1972. xxxiii–xxxvi. Introduction gives best short account of Macaulay.

————. "Thomas Babington Macaulay." In *Victorian Prose: a Guide to Research*, ed. David J. DeLaura, pp. 19–30. New York: The Modern Language Association, 1973. Excellent survey.

CRUIKSHANK, MARGARET. "Macaulay's Speeches in the House of Commons." *Bulletin of Bibliography*, 34 (1977), 134–36.

CUNNINGHAM, DONALD. "Thomas Babington Macaulay: A Bibliography of Twentieth-Century Periodical Articles and Speeches." *Bulletin of Bibliography*, 28 (1971), 19–21.

FRENCH, W. H., AND GERALD SANDERS, EDS. *The Reader's Macaulay*. New York: American Book, 1936. Pp. 21–29. Good introduction.

PINNEY, THOMAS. "Notes on Macaulay's Unacknowledged and Uncollected Writings." *Papers of the Bibliographical Society of America*, 67 (1973), 17–31. A valuable list.

2. Biography and Criticism

ABBOTT, W. C. "Thomas Babington Macaulay: Historian." In *Adventures in Reputation*. Cambridge: Harvard University Press, 1935. Traces decline of his reputation; treats the *History* favorably.

ARNOLD, FREDERICK. *The Public Life of Lord Macaulay*. London: Tinsley Brothers, 1862. Gives more detailed account than Trevelyan's of Macaulay's political career; prints extracts from many speeches and letters.

ARNOLD, MATTHEW. "A French Critic on Milton." In *The Complete Prose Works of Matthew Arnold*. Ed. R. H. Super. Ann Arbor: University of Michigan Press, 1960—. Vol. 8, *Essays Religious and Mixed*, 1972. Macaulay's "Milton" the work of a rhetorician, not a "disinterested critic."

BAGEHOT, WALTER. "Macaulay." *National Review*, 2 (1856), 357–87. One of the best Victorian critiques; discusses Macaulay's "*in*experiencing nature."

BEATTY, R. C. *Lord Macaulay: Victorian Liberal.* Norman: University of Oklahoma Press, 1938. Unsympathetic biography; weak on Victorian background.

BROWNING, ANDREW. "Lord Macaulay 1800–59." *Historical Journal*, 2 (1959), 149–160. Focuses on the *History*.

BUTTERFIELD, HERBERT. *History and Human Relations.* London: Collins, 1951. Discusses Macaulay in the last chapter, "History as a Branch of Literature."

―――. "Reflections on Macaulay." *Listener*, 90 (13 December 1973), 826–27.

CARLETON, WILLIAM G. "Macaulay and the Trimmers." *American Scholar*, 19 (1950), 73–82. Argues that Macaulay essentially is a moderate.

CARVER, GEORGE. "Trevelyan and Macaulay." In *Alms for Oblivion*. Milwaukee: Bruce, 1946. Good analysis of Trevelyan's *Life*.

CLARK, HARRY HAYDEN. "The Vogue of Macaulay in America." *Transactions of the Wisconsin Academy*, 34 (1942), 237–92. Good survey of criticism to 1940.

CLIVE, JOHN. "Macaulay, History, and the Historians." *History Today*, IX (1959), 830–36. Relates Macaulay's personality to his writing.

―――. *Macaulay: the Shaping of the Historian.* New York: Knopf, 1973. The most important work to appear on Macaulay since Trevelyan's *Life* in 1876; uses new sources to describe Macaulay's life to 1839 in its full historical context; reviewed by H. R. Trevor-Roper in *New York Review of Books*, 3 May 1973, pp. 3–5; by Eric Stokes in *New Statesman*, 29 June 1973, pp. 963–64; by Joseph Hamburger in *Reviews in European History*, 1 (1974), 206–14; by M. L. Cruikshank in *Victorian Periodicals Newsletter*, 7 (1974), 15–18; by John M. Robson in *Victorian Studies*, 17 (1974), 327–28; and by G. Kitson Clark in *History and Theory*, 13 (1974), 145–62.

COCKSHUT, A. O. J. *Truth to Life: The Art of Biography in the Nineteenth Century.* London: Collins, 1974. Appraises Trevelyan's life of Macaulay in Chapter 8, pp. 125–43.

COLLIS, JOHN STEWART. "Macaulay After One Hundred Years." *Time and Tide*, 41 (9 January 1960), 29. Macaulay had "unexampled pictorial power."

DAS GUPTA, R. K. "Macaulay's Writings on India." In *Historians of India, Pakistan and Ceylon*, ed. C. H. Philips, pp. 230–40. London: Oxford University Press, 1961. Good defense of the essays on Clive and Hastings.

DAVIES, GODFREY. "The Treatment of Constitutional History in Macaulay's *History of England*." *Huntington Library Quarterly*, 2

(1939), 179–204. Praises Macaulay for seeing full significance of constitutional questions; disputes some of his interpretations.

FIRTH, SIR CHARLES. *A Commentary on Macaulay's History of England.* London: Frank Cass, 1964. First published in 1938; invaluable study; comprehensive and judicious.

FISHER, H. A. L. "The Whig Historians." *Proceedings of the British Academy,* 14 (1928), 297–339. Macaulay's *History* "furnishes the best general introduction to the understanding of English history and English political life which has ever been written."

FONG, DAVID. "Macaulay: the Essayist as Historian." *Dalhousie Review,* 51 (1971), 38–48. Persuasively argues against the sharp distinction usually made between the essays and the *History.*

————. "Macaulay and Johnson." *University of Toronto Quarterly,* 40 (1970), 27–40. Defends Macaulay's criticism of eighteenth century literature by examining late essays.

FORÇADE, EUGÈNE. "Une Révolution Conservatrice." *Revue des Deux Mondes,* 1 September 1849, pp. 769–809. Review of the *History of England,* vols. 1 and 2.

FROUDE, JAMES ANTHONY,"Lord Macaulay." *Frasers,* n.s. 13 (1876), 675–94. Portrays Macaulay as representative Victorian.

GAY, PETER. "Macaulay." In *Style in History.* New York: Basic Books, 1974. Concludes that "readers have taken Macaulay's style as a mirror of his defects rather than of his virtues."

GEYL, PIETER. "Macaulay in his Essays." In *Debates with Historians.* Groningen: J. B. Wolters, 1955. Patronizing survey.

[GLADSTONE, W. E.] Review of Trevelyan's *Life. Quarterly Review,* CXLII (1876), 1–50. Best Victorian essay on Macaulay.

GRETTON, R. H. Introduction to *Five Essays by Lord Macaulay from the Encyclopaedia Britannica.* London: G. Bell, 1914. Finds these last essays Macaulay's best.

GRIFFIN, JOHN R. *The Intellectual Milieu of Lord Macaulay.* Ottawa: University of Ottawa Press, 1965. Useful for emphasizing the liberty theme in Macaulay but weakened by unsubstantiated generalizations.

HAMBURGER, JOSEPH. *Macaulay and the Whig Tradition.* Chicago: University of Chicago Press, 1976. Portrays Macaulay as a trimmer. Persuasively argued.

JEBB, R. C. *Macaulay.* Cambridge: Cambridge University Press, 1900. Originally a lecture; one of the best commentaries on Macaulay; especially good on style.

KELLETT, E. E. "Macaulay's *History.*" *London Quarterly and Holborn Review,* 163 (1938), 289–301. Favorable assessments of Macaulay and Firth's *Commentary.*

KER, W. P. "Macaulay." In *English Prose,* ed. Henry Craik, V, 409–18. London: Macmillan, 1896. Excellent, detailed account of Macaulay's essays.

KNOWLES, DAVID. *Lord Macaulay, 1800–59.* Cambridge: Cambridge University Press, 1960. An appealing essay, more a commemoration than a critical estimate; originally a lecture.

LEVINE, GEORGE. *The Boundaries of Fiction: Carlyle, Macaulay, and Newman.* Princeton: Princeton University Press, 1968. Uses characteristics of the works to show flaws of the man.

MACGREGOR, D. H. *Lord Macaulay.* London: C. J. Clay, 1901. General study; contains good analysis of Macaulay's view of history.

MADDEN, WILLIAM. "Macaulay's Style." *The Art of Victorian Prose.* eds. George Levine and William Madden. New York: Oxford University Press, 1968. Stimulating and original essay.

MAGOUN, FRANCIS P. "Lord Macaulay, a Singer of Tales." *Neuphilologische Mitteilungen,* 73 (1972), 686–89. On stock epithets in *The Lays of Ancient Rome.*

MAURICE, F. D. "Lord Macaulay." *Macmillan's* 1 (1860), 241–47. Good treatment of speeches and *History.*

[MILL, J. S.] "Macaulay's *Lays of Ancient Rome.*" *Westminster Review,* 39 (1843), 55–59. Praises Macaulay's imagination and knowledge of Roman history.

MILLGATE, JANE. "Father and Son: Macaulay's *Edinburgh* Debut." *Review of English Studies,* XXI (1970), 159–67. Argues that Macaulay's first essay was "The West Indies" (1825).

————. "History versus Fiction: Thackeray's Response to Macaulay." *Costerus,* n.s. 2 (1974), 43–58. Influence of Macaulay, especially on *Henry Esmond.*

————. *Macaulay.* London: Routledge and Kegan Paul, 1973. First-rate critical study; comprehensive and illuminating.

————. "Macaulay at Work: an Example of his Use of Sources." *Cambridge Bibliographical Society Transactions,* 5 (1970), 90–98. Excellent article on the Temple essay.

MINTO, WILLIAM. *Manual of English Prose Literature.* Boston: Ginn, 1887. Good section on Macaulay's style, pp. 77–130.

MORGAN, PETER. "Macaulay on Periodical Style." *Victorian Periodicals Newsletter,* 1 (1968), 26–7.

MORLEY, JOHN. "Macaulay." In *Nineteenth Century Essays.* Ed. Peter Stansky. Chicago: University of Chicago Press, 1970. One of the best Victorian essays on Macaulay.

MORTIMER, RAYMOND. "Mighty Opposites." *Cornhill,* 161 (1944), 54–67. On rivalry between Macaulay and Brougham as *Edinburgh* contributors; based on *The Correspondence of Macvey Napier.*

MUNBY, A. N. L. *Macaulay's Library.* Glasgow: Jackson, 1966. Pamphlet on Macaulay's marginalia.

OTTEN, TERRY. "Macaulay's Critical Theory of Imagination and Reason." *Journal of Aesthetics and Art Criticism,* 28 (1969), 33–43. Treats primitivistic ideas in the essays, especially early works.

OURSEL, PAUL. *Les Essais de Lord Macaulay*. Paris: Librarie Hachette, 1882. The only full length critical study of the essays; includes biographical introduction and bibliography.

PAGET, JOHN. *The New Examen*. Manchester: Haworth Press, 1934. First published in 1861; disputes Macaulay's interpretation in the *History* of the Duke of Marlborough, William Penn, the massacre of Glencoe and the highlands of Scotland.

PAUL, HERBERT. "Macaulay and his Critics." In *Men and Letters*. London: John Lane, 1901. Spirited defense of Macaulay; finds his late biographical essays "perfect models of artistic condensation."

POTTER, G. R. *Macaulay*. Writers and Their Works, No. 116. London: Longmans, Green, 1959.

*Review of English Literature*. 1 (October 1960). Macaulay issue. Articles on his historical imagination by John Clive; his style by G. S. Fraser; his poetry by C. V. Wedgwood; and his Indian career by Eric Stokes.

ROGERS, WILLIAM H. "A Study in Contrasts: Carlyle and Macaulay as Book Reviewers." *Florida State University Studies*, 5 (1952), 1–9. Macaulay's "delinquencies as a critic . . . have been grossly exaggerated."

ROWSE, A. L. "Macaulay's Essays." In *Victorian Literature. Modern Essays in Criticism*, ed. Austin Wright. New York: Oxford University Press, 1961. Rather conventional beauties and faults treatment; no suggestion of diversity of the essays.

SAINTSBURY, GEORGE. "Macaulay." In *Corrected Impressions. Essays on Victorian Writers*. London: W. Heinemann, 1885. Patronizing and generally negative evaluation.

SCHUYLER, ROBERT L. "Macaulay and his History—a Hundred Years After." *Political Science Quarterly*, 63 (1948), 161–93. Good treatment of career, personality, and works.

SHIRLEY [JOHN SKELTON]. "A Last Word on Lord Macaulay." *Frasers*, 62 (1860), 438–46. Stresses his moderation.

SIRKIN, GERALD AND NATALIE SIRKIN. "The Battle of Indian Education: Macaulay's Opening Salvo." *Victorian Studies*, XIV (1971), 407–28. Prints letter Macaulay wrote before the famous Minute and gives thorough commentary.

STARZINGER, VINCENT E. *Middlingness: Juste Milieu Political Theory in France and England, 1815–48*. Charlottesville: University of Virginia Press, 1965. Finds more mature Whiggism in the *History* than in the essays.

STEPHEN, LESLIE. "Macaulay." *Cornhill*, 33 (1876), 563–81. Relates Macaulay's defects to general Whig attitudes; vigorous attack on the Whigs.

STIRLING, J. H. *Jerrold, Tennyson and Macaulay*. Edinburgh: Edmonston and Douglas, 1868. Chapter 3, pp. 112–71, traces eighteenth century influences on Macaulay.

STRACHEY, LYTTON. "Macaulay." In *Portraits in Miniature*. London: Chatto and Windus, 1931. Unsympathetic view but concludes that "in power of narration no one has ever surpassed Macaulay."

SVAGLIC, MARTIN. "Classical Rhetoric and Victorian Prose." In *The Art of Victorian Prose*, eds. George Levine and William Madden. New York: Oxford University Press, 1968. Excellent analysis of Macaulay's essay on Milton.

THACKERAY, W. M. "Nil Nisi Bonum." *Cornhill*, 1 (1860), 129–34. Generous tribute to Macaulay.

THOMSON, MARK A. *Macaulay*. The Historical Association Pamphlet No. 42. London: Routledge and Kegan Paul, 1959. Overview stressing the *History;* most valuable of the centenary essays.

TREVELYAN, G. M. *Clio, a Muse*. London: Longmans, 1914. Praises Macaulay but finds his "too great certainty of temper" a weakness.

————. "Macaulay and the Sense of Optimism." In *Ideas and Beliefs of the Victorians*. London: Sylvan Press, 1949. Macaulay's view of progress.

TREVELYAN, G. O. *The Life and Letters of Lord Macaulay*. 2 vols. London: Longman, 1876. One of the best Victorian biographies and the standard life of Macaulay; reprinted 1961 by Oxford University Press.

TREVOR-ROPER, HUGH R. Introduction to *Macaulay. The History of England*. New York: Washington Square Press, 1968.

————. "Macaulay and the Glorious Revolution." In *Men and Events*. New York: Harper, 1957. Brief sketch of Macaulay's characteristics as a writer.

URLIN, R. DENNY. *On the Late Lord Macaulay, his Life and Writings*. Dublin: Hodges, Smith, 1860. Pamphlet.

VALENTI, JACK. "Macaulay and his Critics." In *The Bitter Taste of Glory*. Nine Portraits of Power and Conflict. New York: World Publishing, 1971. Very general, sympathetic assessment.

WEBER, RONALD. "Singer and Seer: Macaulay on the Historian as Poet." *Papers on Language and Literature*, 3 (1967), 210–19. Perceptive reading of three early essays: "Milton," "Dryden," and "History."

WELLS, J. "Macaulay as a Man of Letters." *Fortnightly Review*, 130 (1928), 441–53. Takes issue with negative judgments of Morley, Stephen, and Morison.

WILLIAMS, CHARLES. "Lord Macaulay." In *The Image of the City and Other Essays*. London: Oxford University Press, 1958. Biographical sketch with astute critical comments interspersed.

YODER, EDWIN. "Macaulay Revisited." *South Atlantic Quarterly*, 63 (1964), 542–51. Engagingly written account of the *History*.

# Index

(The Works of Macaulay are listed under his name)

174

**DATE DUE**

| | | | |
|---|---|---|---|
| | | | |
| | | | |
| | | | |
| | | | |
| | | | |
| | | | |
| | | | |
| | | | |
| | | | |
| | | | |
| | | | |
| | | | |
| | | | |
| | | | |
| | | | |
| | | | |

DEMCO 38-297